FUN WITH FELT

ANNETTE FELDMAN

VNR VAN NOSTRAND REINHOLD COMPANY
New York Cincinnati Toronto London Melbourne

In Loving Memory
of
My Parents, Gertrude and Emanuel Gerber
and
My Dear Friend, Ruth Nesbit Lenhoff

and also to
My Husband, Irving
and
Valerie Kurita, my friend and close associate,
and other loyal members of my staff—Antonia
Builes, Bertha Zeltser. Julie Burgess, Julia
Nemar, and Janet McEneaney—without any of
whom the production of this book would not
have been possible.
Photography by Doug Long, Photocraft

Copyright © 1980 by Litton Educational Publishing, Inc.
Library of Congress Catalog Card Number 80-12152
ISBN 0-442-25774-0

Printed in the United States of America.
Designed by Loudan Enterprises
Drawings by Michael Hernandez and Valerie Kurita

Published by Van Nostrand Reinhold Company
A division of Litton Educational Publishing, Inc.
135 West 50th Street, New York, NY 10020, U.S.A.

Van Nostrand Reinhold Limited
1410 Birchmount Road
Scarborough, Ontario M1P 2E7, Canada

Van Nostrand Reinhold Australia Pty. Ltd.
17 Queen Street
Mitcham, Victoria 3132, Australia

Van Nostrand Reinhold Company Limited
Molly Millars Lane
Wokingham, Berkshire, England

16 15 14 13 12 11 10 9 8 7 6 5 4 3 2 1

Library of Congress Cataloging in Publication Data

Feldman, Annette.
  Fun with felt.

  Includes index.
  1. Felt work. I. Title.
TT880.F44   746.'0463   80-12152
ISBN 0-442-25774-0

CONTENTS

INTRODUCTION

For you and for me, sharing this interesting book, felt is for fun. It was because the unusual matted fabric known as felt has such special characteristics that I was able to design the many exciting projects that appear on the pages that follow. And it is because of these same special qualities that you will be able to make all the projects quickly and easily, with pleasure in the doing and pride in the results of your work. Oddly enough, however, although felt is great fun to work with, it came into being under circumstances that, far from being pleasant, were actually associated with a tale of woe.

It seems that in France, far back in the days of Robert the Devil, there was a monk known as St. Feutre, who decided that he must atone for his sins by making a pilgrimage to a far-distant shrine. He started out one bright day with staff in hand, cockleshells in his cap, and a pair of brand-new sandals made by the abbey cobbler on his feet. The trip was a long and arduous one, but with penance strong in his heart St. Feutre travelled steadfastly along his way, leaving early each morning from the inn or mission where he had slept the night before, and walking until nightfall before stopping again to rest.

As the days passed, his feet, unaccustomed to the new sandals, became very sore. The monk tried to accept his suffering as a penance and, through prayer, to rid his mind of all thoughts of pain. But with each new step the pain became more difficult to bear, and when he happened to pass a flock of sheep being herded to market, the thought came to him that if only he could put some wool into his sandals, the soft fleece would ease his tread and help to relieve the soreness of his feet. In an instant, thought became deed. He plucked several handfuls of wool and placed them inside his shoes. He felt relief immediately and, praying that God would not be offended by his action, but instead would bless it by showing him a miracle of some sort, St. Feutre continued on his journey in comfort.

Some days later he reached his destination, the Shrine of St. Aubert, and as he pulled off his sandals he became aware that God had indeed performed a miracle. The fluffy sheep's wool he had placed in the sole of each shoe was gone, and in its place was a piece of cloth unlike any that had ever been seen before. Molded to the shape of his foot, it was firm and strong, yet smooth and soft in hand, and it had been created by his own footsteps, daily tramping down and matting the wool inside his shoes into fabric.

So it was that St. Feutre's heaven-sent innersoles became the first things ever made of felt, the matted nonwoven material with which I hope you will have fun as you start to make some of the projects in this book.

You, of course, won't have to trod on your own raw wool as St. Feutre did, because that job has long since been taken over by machines, and you can buy all the felt you want—in several weights and just about any color you are looking for—at any local fabric or department store, although when you do purchase a length of felt, you might remember St. Feutre and give him your silent thanks because it was through his experience that felting was established as one of the most ancient forms of making fabric.

Even though many centuries have passed and much technological progress has been made since the time when our monk dragged his poor aching feet on that long journey of atonement, the principle of manufacturing felt remains the same now as it was then. The process of felt making involves applying heat, moisture, pressure, and friction to wool fibers to create a matted fabric, and it depends on the natural tendency of wool to shrink into springlike coils and interlock to form a dense mat, much the same process as St. Feutre worked out by pounding and rubbing against the pure raw wool in his shoes with his hot, perspiring feet. Felt is still made of wool, or of a combination of wool and fur or hair, although today cotton, rayon, silk, and other "nonfelting" fibers are often blended in with the wool, and the heat, moisture, friction, and pressure required to felt the fibers into a mat are applied mechanically in a carefully controlled way.

Felt manufacture, like that of all woolen fabrics, begins when the sheep are sheared and the fleeces are separated into different grades of wool. After this, the raw wool is scoured (or washed) to remove oil and dirt, then blended and carded, this last process, is one in which the fibers are mechanically combed until they are more or less parallel and form a web about 80 inches wide. After this stage, the process of turning the wool into woven or knitted fabrics is very different from that for making it into felt. For ordinary fabrics, the carded fibers are separated into strands that are then spun into yarn, which is later woven or knitted into fabric. For felt, on the other hand, lengths of the full 80-inch-wide carded-fiber webs are lifted off the machine and layered one on top of the other, mattress-like, until the layers are the proper weight for making felt of the desired thickness (and the finished felt may be as thin as 1/32 inch or as thick as 3 inches). Now the "mattress" of carded webs undergoes a treatment known as hardening, in which it is moistened, steamed, and passed between vibrating plates that tangle the fibers into a mat. At this point, the material can be dried and finished for use as soundproofing or insulation, but it isn't yet very strong because the fibers have not locked together sufficiently, and it must undergo several additional treatments before it will be the kind of felt you'll use to make the projects in this book.

The next step in the journey from fiber to felt is called fulling, or felting, and it is the one in which the fibers really become bonded together into felt. The process involves shrinking the fiber mat into a firm, strong fabric by another controlled application of moisture, heat, and pressure, this time with the addition of soap or a similar chemical lubricant—and if you've ever washed a woolen blanket or garment with the wrong soap in water that was too hot only to have it turn into a boardlike material perhaps half its original size, then you've accidentally accomplished what the fulling process purposefully does.

After fulling, the felt is washed, dyed, and—depending on what its final use will be—it may be sized for extra body, or treated to make it waterproof, flameproof, or mildew resistant. Finally, it is dried on special machines that stretch it to the desired width, and then sheared or pressed between heated rollers to give the surfaces a smooth, lustrous appearance.

And so we have felt—threadless, grainless, nonraveling, strong, warm, resilient, versatile—felt for many important industrial and commercial purposes ranging from insulating airplanes and soundproofing theaters to cushioning piano keys and filtering respirators, and felt to make into clothes and toys and home accessories for our own fun and enjoyment.

I.
FELT FOR FUN

Those of you who have used felt before certainly know what a joy it is to work with, and I hope that the exciting projects and design ideas offered in this book will provide you with fresh stimulation for making many more new things. If you have never done handwork with this material before, *Fun with Felt* will show you how to use it and introduce you to the pleasantly different experience of being able to make lovely things with a minimum of time, effort, and expense.

With felt you can ignore most of the standard preparatory and finishing steps that woven and knitted fabrics normally require. For example, since felt has no grain, you don't have to straighten the material before you use it, and you can lay out your pattern pieces in any direction you wish in order to get the most from your yardage. Nor has felt any threads that can ravel or fray, and edges will always remain as neat and firm as when you cut them, freeing you of the trouble of hemming, facing raw edges, or overcasting seam allowances, the tedious aspects of finishing that so often make a project seem more a chore than a pleasure; yet the very same characteristics that allow you to simplify the process of joining pieces and to eliminate edge finishes entirely also afford you the opportunity to use some very unusual and attractive techniques for seaming and edging that are difficult or impractical to do with ordinary fabrics. In this way, the pieces of a felt project can be joined with either ordinary hand- or machine-stitched seaming or by simply whipstitching the edges together, and the cut edges (both visible and concealed) left raw; or seams can be made and edges embellished with attractive embroidered and crocheted work; the techniques for several of these interesting finishes are described in Chapter 3.

A fascinating material to work with, there is practically no end to the versatility of felt, and the chapters that follow are filled with a wonderful group of designs for all kinds of different things made of felt, each one accompanied by simple-to-follow instructions. It is great fun to use felt for making fashion items such as the vest, tabard, cape, and skating skirt you'll find in Chapter 2; and not only is this unique material available in a full range of colors, easy to work with, and warm and comfortable to wear, but the 72-inch width of the goods will allow you to cut an entire garment in one piece or at most in a few large sections, thus minimizing the number of seams you'll have to stitch.

Felt is perfect for patchwork because of the ease with which the pieces can be joined, and in Chapter 3 you'll find several interesting patchwork projects to make, along with many design ideas to whet your own creative imagination. Then, too, as you will see when you look through the charming designs in Chapter 6, felt is excellent for appliqué work and trimmings—you'll never have the troublesome task of turning under the raw edges of appliqués cut from felt, and affixing them to the project you want to trim requires nothing more than a little glue, fusible bonding material, or simple hand or machine topstitching.

With its firm body and smooth, lustrous finish, felt is also very well suited for making desk sets, lamp bases, tablecloths, wall hangings, and many other kinds of decorative home accessories, all of which you will see as you turn the pages of Chapter 5. And I think the greatest pleasure of all is the one you'll get in discovering that felt works up into the most wonderful toys and Christmas decorations. In Chapter 4 there are toys to delight any child fortunate enough to receive them, including a very special three-car choo-choo train, a cheerful duck puppet who practically quacks when you manipulate him, and a soft pussy cat pillow for a little sleepyhead to rest on. Chapter 7 is filled with holiday decorating ideas that are fresh and new, but packed with memories for all of you who will never forget your very first precious Christmas stocking filled with candy canes and other surprises, the around-the-tree rug piled high with presents, or the little angel you always insisted on being allowed to hang on the tree just as high up as you could reach.

The "Guide to Perfect Work" at the end of the book offers helpful information about how to work with felt, including advice on preparing and cutting it, enlarging and reducing patterns, transferring pattern markings, applying felt appliqués, and apropos of this, I would like to mention here, too, that where instructions for a project call for using bonding material or for using glue, it is because I have found that particular method best for affixing one piece of felt to another in the specific project being shown; however, should you prefer hand sewing to glueing or bonding, a simple whipstitch will do the job and you should feel free to substitute it; and similarly, where I have specified sewing as the preferred method, you may substitute glueing or bonding if you choose, and achieve nearly identical results. It is also important to point out here that the type of felt called for in the materials list for each project is always the average over-the-counter thickness of 1/16 inch, and where yardage is specified, I am referring to the usual 72-inch width; Any of the projects that you make can be sprayed with Scotchgard Fabric Protector to preserve them and keep them fresh-looking for a very long time.

Finally, I'd like you to know that all of the projects and designs made from St. Feutre's miracle fabric have been created especially for this book, and I do hope that as you turn the pages you will find a source of many hours of pleasure—at least as many as I have had in putting them together for you.

2. FASHION

Felt is fun to use for making fashionable clothing and accessories. All of us enjoy wearing things that are attractive and becoming to us, but there's an even more special kind of enjoyment that comes from making those things ourselves and knowing that what we have made is just a little different because we've put our own hand to it. Those of you who are about to enter my own little "specialty shop," whose racks will be displayed on the pages that follow, will find still more pleasure in discovering a group of very interesting fashion items that you won't find in the wardrobe of anyone who hasn't visited the shop. The "main floor" is stocked with accessories, and one flight up you'll find fashion attire—all designed in felt especially for the shop.

Clear instructions are given for making each of the pieces, and where size changes are necessary, you'll be told how to make them. Attractive appliqué motifs, patchwork designs, and embroidered and crocheted edgings have been used to trim a number of the projects you'll find in this exclusive little shop. If you prefer, however, you might enjoy substituting appliqués from among the portfolio of trims in Chapter 6, or patchwork designs from the geometric section of Chapter 3; and you might want to try some of the other edgings described in the edgings and joinings sections of Chapter 3. You can also create many different effects by selecting colors other than those used to make the samples on display. There is room for the play of your own imagination in all the fashions that appear here, and although I hope you'll like them just as they are, I also hope you will feel free to make any changes that you think will please you even more.

HEART-SHAPED AMULET

Embroidered with a delicate tracery of pretty flowers, the amulet shown here is a charming accessory to wear around your neck and a handy little thing, too, for carrying a key, a small vial of perfume, or perhaps a little "mad money."

Materials
- scrap of white felt
- 1¼ yds. narrow black cord or braid
- red, aqua, and green embroidery thread
- black and white sewing thread
- embroidery needle

To Make

Trace the pattern for the amulet and, using it as a guide, cut two heart-shaped pieces from the white felt.

Embroider one of the hearts with flowers, vines, and leaves, using French knots, daisy stitches, and straight stitches as shown on the pattern. Work the leaves and vines with green embroidery thread, and the flowers with red and aqua thread as shown.

Sew the two hearts together, right sides out, with a running stitch, leaving the top portion open. Cut a piece of black cord long enough to fit around the edges of the heart, and stitch it in place, sewing it to the embroidered heart only around the open top portion of the piece. Then stitch together the ends of the remaining length of black cord, and tack the joined ends securely to the inside edge of the embroidered heart at the center top of the piece.

Amulet pattern (actual size)

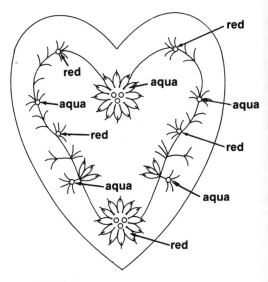

stitch key:
- − = **straight stitch**
- ○ = **French knot**
- ⋂ = **daisy stitch**

COLORFUL PATCHWORK BELT AND PURSE

Angle-shaped patches are used to trim this lace-up-the-front belt and the coordinated detachable bag that hooks on to it. The belt can be made to fit any size (the one shown here is for a 29-inch waist), and you might find it fun to make a pair of them, one for yourself and one for your young daughter.

Materials

- ¼ yd. 72"-wide black felt
- ¼ yd. 72"-wide aqua felt
- scraps of red felt
- ¼ yd. 45"-wide interfacing
- 1 yd. fusible bonding material
- ½ yd. narrow black piping
- 1 yd. narrow black lacing cord
- eyelet kit with 10 ⅛" black eyelets
- 1 large snap fastener
- black and aqua sewing thread
- white glue

To Make

Enlarge the pattern pieces for the purse and belt to full size (instructions for enlarging are given in Chapter 8). From black felt, cut one purse flap following the outline of the pattern, one strip 6 inches wide by 28 inches long (or 1 inch less than your actual waist measurement) for the belt, and one each of the two black patches for the purse front following the outlines of the appropriate patterns for these; from aqua, cut one main purse piece following the outline of the pattern, and, using the appropriate pattern, one patch for the purse flap, and two of each of the three patches for the belt; and from red, one patch for the purse front, one patch for the purse flap, and two each of the two patches for the belt. From interfacing, cut one main purse piece and one purse front, and a strip 3 inches wide and the same length as the black felt strip for the belt. Finally, cut a piece of bonding material in the same shape as each of the patches.

To finish the belt, center the interfacing on the strip of black felt and glue it in place. Fold the long edges of the felt to the wrong side so they meet at the center, and glue them down or seam them together with whipstitches. Overcast the center front edges of the belt with whipstitches. Place each of the aqua and red patches on top of the appropriate pieces of bonding material and, using the belt pattern as a guide, position them on the right side of the belt and bond them in place with an iron as directed on the package of bonding material. Finally, set the ten eyelets in place as shown, and lace the cord through.

To finish the purse, glue the interfacing to one side of the main purse piece. Repeat for the purse front. Then place the two interfaced pieces together, right sides out, insert the piping between the layers as an edging, and stitch the pieces together around the curved outer edge, taking care to sew through all layers. Glue the black flap piece in place on the outside of the purse. Place the patches on top of the appropriate pieces of bonding material and adhere them to the purse front and the flap in the positions shown on the patterns. Finally, fold the purse flap along the fold line and sew the snap fastener in place for the closing.

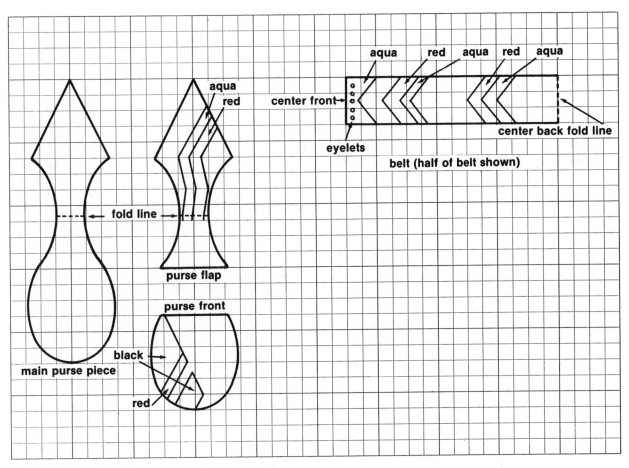

Pattern pieces for belt and purse (1 square = 1″)

FANCY SUSPENDERS AND FLOWER-PETALED CAP

Many of us can remember being very young and bubbling with excitement when we were allowed to dress up in our Tyrolean suspenders and cap. Members of today's kindergarten set will feel the very same way on those special days when they trade their jeans and T-shirts for party clothes and this charming set of felt accessories.

Materials

- ¼ yd. 72"-wide red felt
- ¼ yd. 72"-wide white felt
- scraps of aqua and green felt
- 4 suspender grips
- red and white sewing thread
- white glue
- pinking shears
- hole puncher

To Make

Trace and enlarge to full size the patterns for the cross piece and shoulder strap of the suspenders, and the pattern for the cap (instructions for enlarging are given in Chapter 8). Trace the petal and leaf patterns for the large and small flowers.

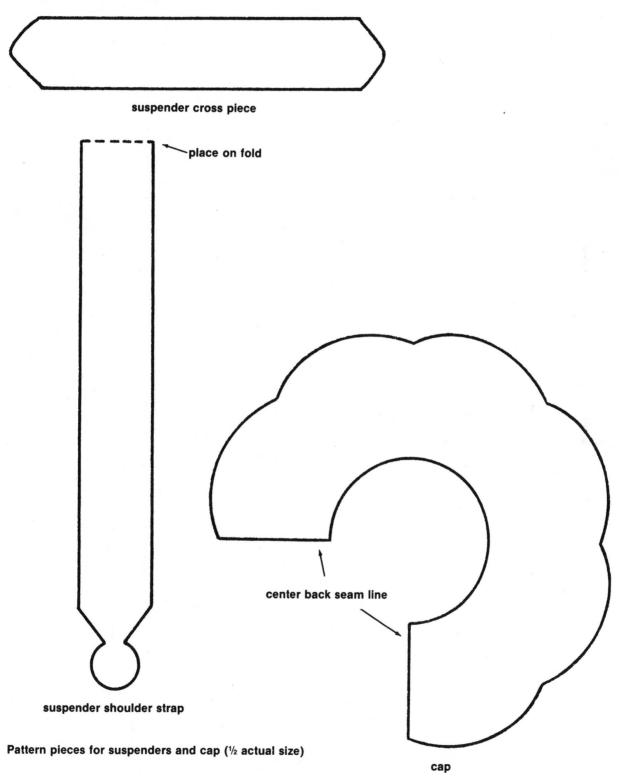

suspender cross piece

place on fold

suspender shoulder strap

center back seam line

cap

Pattern pieces for suspenders and cap (½ actual size)

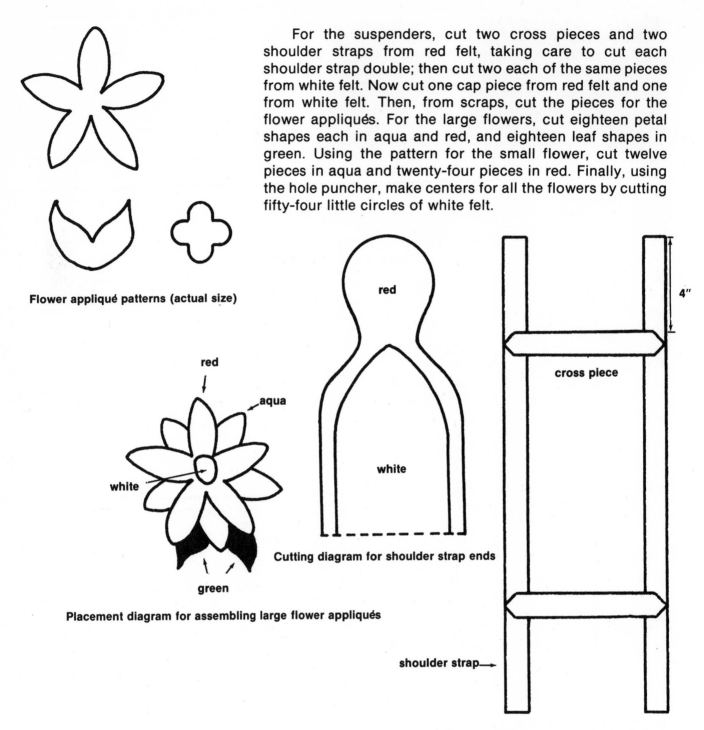

For the suspenders, cut two cross pieces and two shoulder straps from red felt, taking care to cut each shoulder strap double; then cut two each of the same pieces from white felt. Now cut one cap piece from red felt and one from white felt. Then, from scraps, cut the pieces for the flower appliqués. For the large flowers, cut eighteen petal shapes each in aqua and red, and eighteen leaf shapes in green. Using the pattern for the small flower, cut twelve pieces in aqua and twenty-four pieces in red. Finally, using the hole puncher, make centers for all the flowers by cutting fifty-four little circles of white felt.

Flower appliqué patterns (actual size)

red

aqua

white

green

Placement diagram for assembling large flower appliqués

red

white

Cutting diagram for shoulder strap ends

4″

cross piece

shoulder strap→

Placement diagram for assembling suspender pieces

To assemble the suspenders, pink the edges of the two white cross pieces with a pinking shears, trimming away ⅜ inch on all sides. Pink the two white suspender straps in the same manner, but trim off the round ends entirely, as shown in the diagram of the shoulder strap ends. Center the white cross pieces and shoulder straps on the larger red ones and glue them down. Arrange the cross pieces and shoulder straps as shown in the placement diagram and sew them together. Then sew on the suspender grips.

To assemble the cap, pink the scalloped edges of the white cap piece, trimming away ⅜ inch all around (do not pink the edges of the center back seam). Then center the white cap piece on the red one and glue it down. Complete the center back seam by sewing the edges together with a whipstitch.

Assemble the eighteen large flowers by glueing together one leaf, one of each of the red and aqua petal shapes, and one little white circle as shown in the placement diagram for the large flower. Complete the small flowers by glueing a white circle in the center of each of the small aqua and red petal shapes. Arrange the large and small flowers on the cap and suspenders as shown in the flower placement diagram and glue them in place.

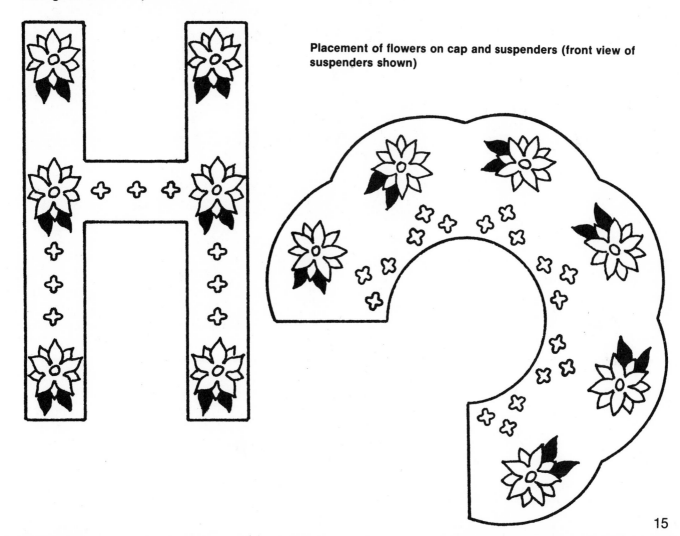

Placement of flowers on cap and suspenders (front view of suspenders shown)

BERET AND MATCHING ASCOT

This simple wear-it-everywhere beret is shown teamed with a matching ascot that's been personalized with a bold monogram in a contrasting color. The set is easy to make and requires only a small amount of material, but it is so fashionable you may want to make several sets—a few in different colors for yourself, and some to give as gifts for friends.

Materials

- ½ yd. 72"-wide white felt
- scraps of black felt
- 2 small snap fasteners
- white sewing thread
- white glue

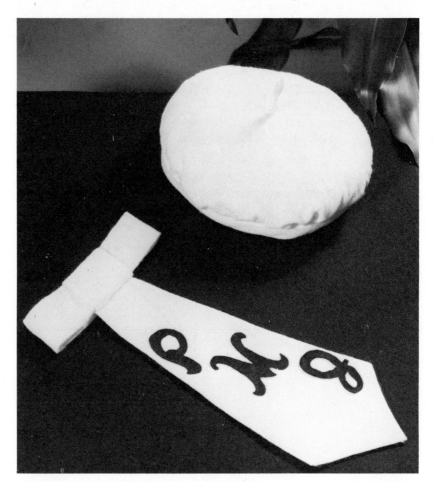

To Make

Enlarge the pattern for the ascot to full size (instructions for enlarging are given in Chapter 8).

For the beret, from white felt cut a circle 12 inches in diameter, a strip measuring 3 inches by 23 inches (or the desired headband size), and a strip ¼ inch by 3½ inches for the trim.

For the ascot, from white felt cut one piece following the outline of the ascot pattern, and a strip measuring 3 inches by 13½ inches (or the desired neckband size). Then from black, cut the initials for your monogram, using the block or script letter patterns in Chapter 6 and enlarging the letters to the size you want.

To make the beret, run a gathering stitch around the felt circle ¼ inch in from the edge, and gather the circle to fit your head. With a whipstitch, sew together the two short ends of the headband strip. Fold the headband in half, aligning the two long cut edges. Then insert the gathered edge of the circle into the folded headband, arranging the gathers evenly and adjusting the size of the circle to fit the headband. Stitch the headband to the circle, sewing through all three layers. Now fold the headband in half again to the outside, and sew the folded top edges in place. Finally, cut a ⅛-inch slit at the very center of the beret, insert the two ends of the small trimming strip through the slit, and tack them to the underside of the beret.

To make the ascot, begin by clipping the side seam allowances as indicated on the pattern, cutting just up to the side seam fold lines. Next, fold the side and bottom seam allowances of the tie portion of the piece to the wrong side and glue them in place. Then fold the side seam allowances of the neckband casing to the right side of the piece and glue them in place. Fold the top edge of the neckband casing to the right side along the top fold line, fold the casing down again along the bottom fold line, and whip the new folded bottom edge to the tie. Fold the felt strip for the neckband in half lengthwise, whip the cut edges together, and slip the neckband through the neckband casing of the ascot. To make the closure, sew the snap fasteners to the open back ends of the neckband. Finally, arrange your initials on the tie as shown in the photograph, and glue them in place.

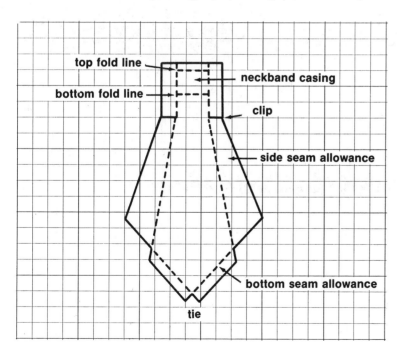

Ascot pattern (1 square = 1″)

TOTE BAG

Made in red and trimmed with snowflake appliqués in a contrasting color, this tote bag is a fashionable variation of the usual handy but ordinary-looking tote. Big, roomy, and comfortable to carry, it is not only attractive but, like all the projects in this book, is easy to make as well.

Materials
- ½ yd. 72"-wide red felt
- ¼ yd. 72"-wide black felt
- ½ yd. interfacing
- ½ yd. lining material
- 2 2"-in-diameter black plastic rings
- 3 1⅛" round black buttons
- 1 large snap fastener
- red sewing thread
- white glue

To Make

Enlarge the pattern pieces for the tote bag and flap to full size (instructions for enlarging are given in Chapter 8), and trace the pattern for the snowflake trim.

From red felt, cut two main bag pieces and two flaps, following the outlines of the patterns; then cut one 3-inch by 37-inch strip for the gusset, and two 3-inch by 32-inch strips for the strap. From black felt, cut five complete snowflake shapes, and then cut three three-armed partial snowflakes as indicated by the shaded portion of the snowflake pattern. Finally, cut two main bag pieces and one gusset strip from both the lining material and the interfacing.

Arrange the eight snowflakes on one of the main bag pieces as shown in the placement diagram and glue them down. Trim the three interfacing pieces ⅛ inch around all edges, center them on the wrong side of the corresponding felt pieces, and glue them in place. Then, with the pieces right side out, stitch the main sections of the bag to the gusset strip, sewing by hand or by machine ⅛ inch in from the edge and leaving a 1-inch end of the gusset strip extending beyond the top of the bag at each side to make tabs for the rings. Draw the extended gusset ends through the black plastic rings and stitch them in place.

Place the two strap pieces together and stitch around all four sides ⅛ inch in from the edge. Draw one end of the strap through each ring of the bag and knot it in place as shown in the photograph. Finish the flap of the bag by placing the two flap pieces together, right sides out, and stitching around all sides ⅛ inch in from the edge. Trim one side of the flap with the three black buttons. Then stitch the flap in place along the center top of the untrimmed back section of the bag, and sew the snap fastener to the front section of the bag and to the underside of the flap.

To make the lining, sew the gusset and main lining pieces together ¼ inch in from the edge. Then trim the extended ends of the gusset flush with the top of the main sections, turn the entire top edge ¼ inch to the wrong side, and hem. Finally, insert the finished lining, wrong side out, into the bag, and stitch it to the inside of the bag around the top edge.

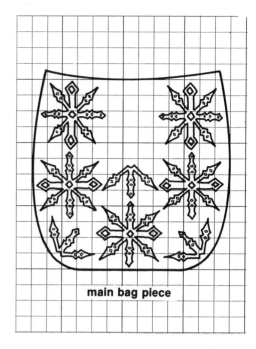

main bag piece

Pattern pieces for tote bag (1 square = 1″) and placement of snowflake trim

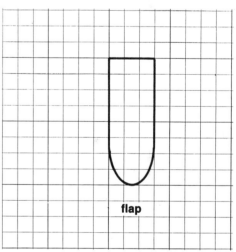

flap

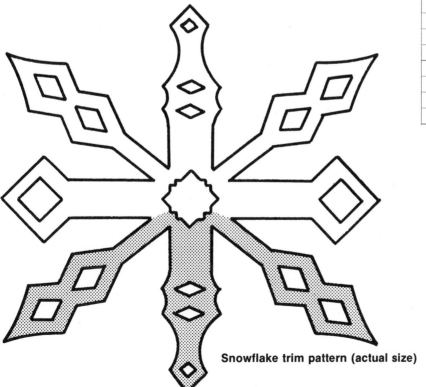

Snowflake trim pattern (actual size)

SLIPPERS FOR EVERYONE

Made from just two pairs of innersoles, a few scraps of felt, and a little knitting yarn, these slippers take only a few minutes to put together and can be made in any size. They're comfortable to wear and are great for gift giving.

Materials

- 3" x 21" piece of aqua felt
- 3" x 21" piece of white felt
- 3" x 21" piece of black felt
- 2 pairs of plastic-lined innersoles in desired size
- small amount of black medium-weight knitting yarn
- brown sewing thread
- Duco cement
- Size G crochet hook

To Make

From the felt, cut four ¾-inch by 21-inch strips in each of the three colors. Make four three-strand braids, using one felt strip of each color for each braid, and temporarily secure the braid ends with paper clips or safety pins.

Placing your foot on one of the innersoles, crisscross two of the braids over your foot as shown in the photograph, and measure the exact length you'll need for a comfortable fit. Cut the braids to these lengths, discarding the excess, and tack the braid ends securely with thread. Repeat the procedure to prepare the two braids for the other slipper.

Position one set of braids on the nonplastic-lined side of one innersole (this will be the bottom innersole of the slipper), and sew the braid ends in place securely. Then, keeping the plastic side up, glue the top innersole of the pair to the bottom one, enclosing the tacked braid ends. Repeat the procedure to assemble the other slipper.

To finish the slippers, crochet two chains with the knitting yarn, each one long enough to fit around the edge of a slipper, and then glue the chains in place.

SELF-FRINGED SHAWL WITH APPLIQUÉD POCKET

This stunning shawl, appropriate at any time of day when you need a little something to throw over your shoulders for warmth, is made from a single length of felt and needs no seaming or hemming. It is trimmed at both ends with fringe cut into the felt in graduated lengths, and has an attractive Art Deco patchwork pocket.

Materials
- 2/3 yd. 72"-wide aqua felt
- small amount of white medium-weight knitting yarn
- aqua sewing thread
- Size G crochet hook

To Make

Trace the patch pattern for the pocket trim. From the aqua felt, cut a 12-inch by 72-inch piece for the shawl, one 8½-inch square for the pocket, and eight patches for the Art Deco pocket trim.

21

Cut ⅜-inch-wide strips of fringe along each short end of the shawl piece, graduating the length of the strips as shown in the cutting and placement diagram. Arrange the patches on the pocket piece as shown in the same diagram and glue them in place. Then, with the white yarn, crochet chains long enough to outline the edges of all the patches, and glue the chains in place as shown in the photograph. Now position the trimmed pocket near one end of the shawl as shown, and stitch it in place. Finally, crochet two chains, one long enough to fit around the side and bottom edges of the pocket and the other one long enough to fit around the two long edges and just inside the cutting line of the fringe at each end of the shawl, and sew these chains in place.

Patch pattern for pocket trim (actual size)

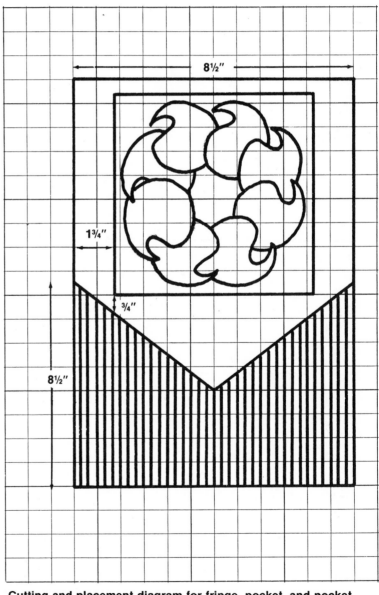

Cutting and placement diagram for fringe, pocket, and pocket trim pieces (1 square = 1″)

TABARD FOR FASHION AND WARMTH

Easy to wear and easy to make, the tabard shown here is pocketed and fringed, and embroidered around the edges with a self-color blanket stitch. It can be made in small (32-34), medium (36-38), or large (40-42) size, and sizing instructions are included in the directions.

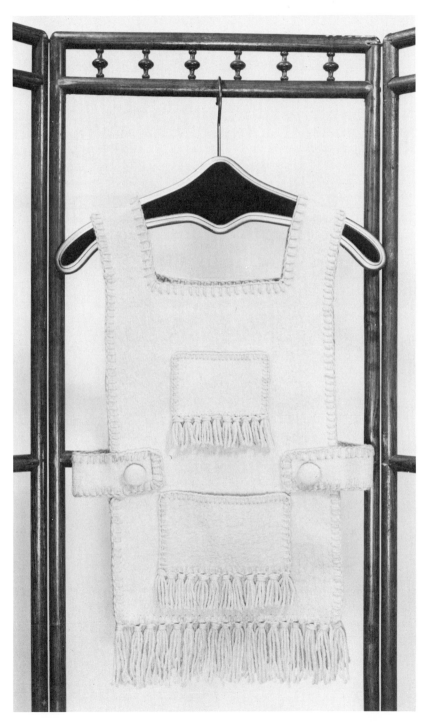

Materials
- ½ yd. 72"-wide aqua felt
- 4 oz. aqua medium-weight knitting yarn
- 2 1⅛" round button molds
- aqua sewing thread
- large-eyed embroidery needle

To Make

Enlarge the pattern for the tabard to full size, using the continuous-line markings to make a small size, the dotted-line markings to make a medium size, or the broken-line markings to make a large size (instructions for enlarging are given in Chapter 8).

From the aqua felt, cut two main body pieces following the outline of the tabard pattern, one 3¼-inch by 5-inch rectangle for the small pocket, one 4½-inch by 7-inch rectangle for the large pocket, two 2¼-inch by 10-inch strips for the side tabs, and two 1¾-inch-in-diameter circles to cover the button molds.

Sew the two main body pieces together at the shoulders. Then with the black yarn, embroider blanket stitches around all the edges of the tabard, pockets, and tabs, as shown in the section on embroidered edgings and joinings in Chapter 3.

To trim the tabard with fringe, cut a number of 8-inch strands of yarn, and then knot a group of three strands through every other blanket stitch along the bottom front and bottom back edges. Fringe the bottom edge of each pocket in the same way, using 5-inch strands for the large pocket and 4-inch strands for the small pocket.

Position the pockets and the tabs on the tabard as shown on the pattern, and sew them in place. Finally, cover each button mold with one of the felt circles as directed on the button mold package, and sew the decorative buttons in position on the tabs as shown in the photograph.

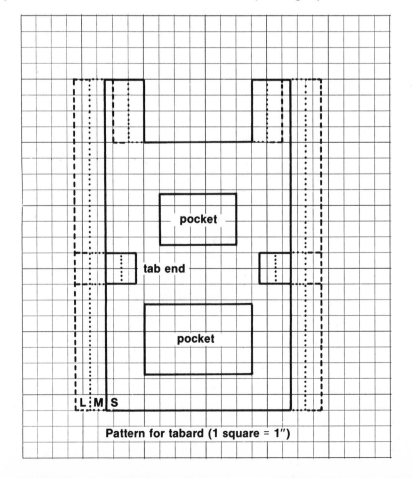

Pattern for tabard (1 square = 1″)

HIS AND HER VESTS

Both of these red vests are bright and fun to wear. The one for her is open down the front and closes with a bow at the neckline, while the one for him buttons down the front in traditional fashion. Both have rounded bottom corners and decorative patch pockets, and each is trimmed in black with crochet stitches worked through an embroidered edging. Each vest can be made in a small, medium, or large size.

Materials for Each Vest
- 2/3 yd. 72"-wide red felt
- 4 oz. black medium-weight knitting yarn
- 5 ½" round black buttons (for His Vest only)
- red sewing thread
- large-eyed embroidery needle
- Size F crochet hook

To Make Her Vest

Enlarge the pattern for the woman's vest to full size, using the continuous-line markings to make a small size, the dotted-line markings to make a medium size, or the broken-line markings to make a large size (instructions for enlarging are given in Chapter 8).

Fold the felt double, place the vest pattern on the fold line as indicated, and cut out the vest, cutting through two thicknesses. Then cut two pocket pieces, following the outline of the pocket pattern.

Stitch the vest together at the shoulders, sewing by hand or by machine ¼ inch in from the edge. Then embroider blanket stitches around the edges of the entire piece, including the armholes, as shown in the section on embroidered edgings and joinings in Chapter 3, except for this case make each stitch a double one by working one blanket stitch and then making a second blanket stitch in the same spot. Crochet a shell stitch edging through the blanket stitches as shown in the section on crocheted edgings and joinings in Chapter 3, for this project working the edging pattern through the tops of every other blanket stitch. Edge the pockets in the same manner, then position them on the vest as shown on the pattern, and sew them in place. Finally, crochet two 15-inch chains and sew them in place for a neckline tie.

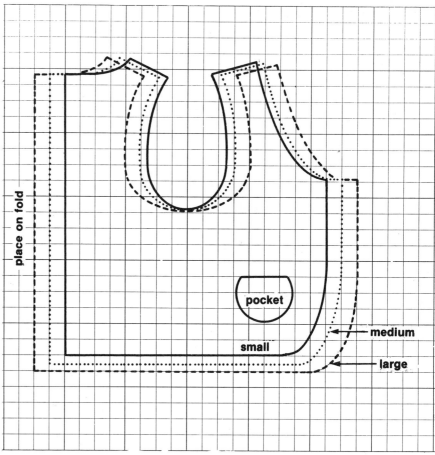

Pattern for woman's vest (1 square = 1")

To Make His Vest

Using the pattern for the man's vest, enlarge the pattern, cut out the vest and pockets, stitch the shoulder seams, and work a blanket stitch edging around the entire piece and around the pockets following the directions for Her Vest. Then work a single crochet edging through the blanket stitches following the directions for this edging given in Chapter 3. Position the pockets on the vest as shown on the pattern, and sew them in place. Work five ⅝-inch buttonholes by hand or by machine along the left front edge of the vest, positioning them as shown on the pattern. Finish by sewing the five buttons in corresponding positions along the right front edge of the vest.

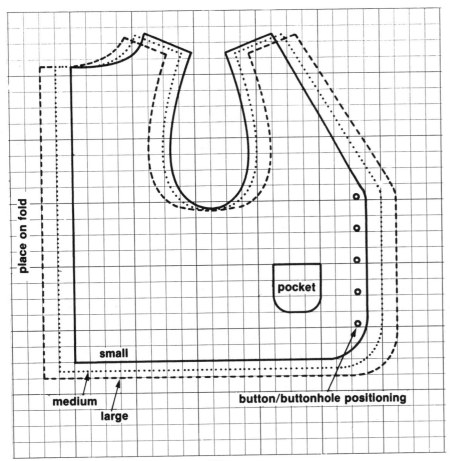

Pattern for man's vest (1 square = 1")

YOUNG BALLERINA'S SKATING SKIRT

With its gay appliquéd hearts and flowers and its bouncy red ball fringe, this very special skating skirt will help any young ballerina to waltz merrily around the skating rink. The skirt, seamless and cut from a length of spanking white felt, is 10½ inches long and has a 20-inch waist measurement. It is made to fit a child who wears a Size 4-5, but instructions are also given in parentheses for making it in a Size 6-7 with a 24-inch waistline.

Materials

- 1 yd. 72"-wide white felt
- scraps of red, turquoise, yellow, kelly green, and black felt
- 2¾ (3) yds. medium-size red ball fringe
- 5" zipper
- 2 small snap fasteners
- white and red sewing thread
- white glue

To Make

Enlarge the pattern for the skating skirt appliqués to full size (instructions for enlarging are given in Chapter 8). From white felt, cut a circle measuring 28 (32) inches in diameter for the skirt, and a strip measuring 3½ inches by 21 (25) inches for the waistband; then, using the color keys on the patterns as guides, cut the pieces for one heart appliqué, two birds, two of each of the flowers, and six scrolls from felt scraps of the appropriate color.

To prepare the waistline of the skirt, cut out a circle measuring 5¾ (7) inches in diameter from the center of the large felt circle. Now, starting anywhere along the waistline edge, cut a 5-inch slit for the center back zipper, taking care to make the slit perpendicular to the waistline and hem edges. Insert the zipper into the slit following the directions on the zipper package. Fold the waistband in half lengthwise and insert the waistline edge of the skirt ½ inch into the long open edges of the waistband, extending one end of the waistband 1 inch beyond the edge of the center back opening. Hand or machine stitch the waistband to the skirt, sewing through all three layers, and then seam each of the short ends of the band. Sew the snap fasteners to the ends of the waistband.

Arrange the appliqués on the skirt as shown in the placement diagram and glue them in place. Glue a pompon cut from the ball fringe at each curve of the scrolls. Finally, stitch the ball fringe around the bottom edge of the skirt.

Placement diagram for skating skirt appliqués

Pattern pieces for skating skirt appliqués (1 square = 1″)

29

PATCHES MAKE A SKIRT

A length of felt, appliquéd with twenty-four square patches in a contrasting color, is sewed to a contrasting-color "yoke" to create this unusual skirt. The one shown here was made in a small (24-inch waist/32-inch hip) size, but instructions are also given in parentheses for making it in a medium (28-inch waist/36-inch hip) size, and in a large (32-inch waist/40-inch hip) size.

Materials

- ¾ yd. 72"-wide white felt
- ¾ yd. 72"-wide aqua felt
- 4 oz. black medium-weight knitting yarn
- 2 black frog fasteners
- 2 ⅞" black buttons
- 3 small snap fasteners
- white, aqua, and black sewing thread
- Size F crochet hook

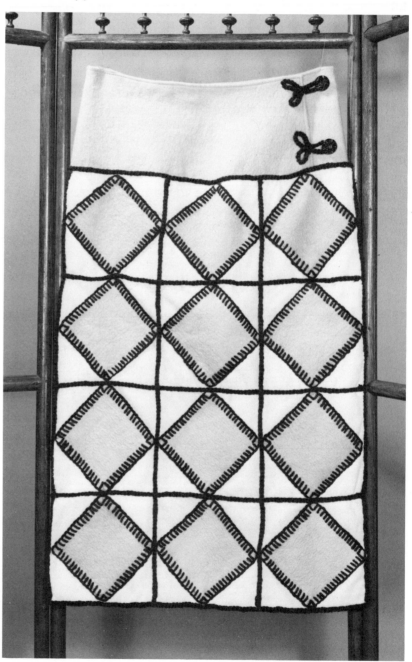

To Make

Enlarge the pattern for the yoke to full size, using the continuous-line markings to make a small size, the dotted-line markings to make a medium size, or the broken-line markings to make a large size (instructions for enlarging are given in Chapter 8).

From white felt, cut a piece measuring 24½ (25, 27½) inches by 35½ (37¾, 40¾) inches for the skirt. From aqua felt, cut one "yoke" piece following the outline of the pattern, and transfer the pattern markings for the side seam lines to the wrong side of the felt (instructions for transferring pattern markings are given in Chapter 8). Then cut twenty-four 3¾ (4¼, 4¾)-inch squares for the patches from the aqua felt.

With the black knitting yarn, embroider a blanket stitch edging around the four sides of each patch as shown in the section on embroidered edgings and joinings in Chapter 3. Arrange the patches on the white felt piece for the skirt as shown in the placement diagram, leaving a ⅝-inch seam allowance along the top and both side edges, and stitch them in place. To mark the right side seam line, make a tiny clip at the midpoint of the edge of the top (yoke) seam allowance.

To trim the skirt, crochet five chains with the black yarn, each one measuring 35 (37, 40) inches. Arrange these chains horizontally between the patches as shown in the placement diagram, allowing the ends of the chains to extend into the side seam allowances, and sew them in place. Then crochet six chains, each one measuring 24 (24½, 27) inches, and one chain measuring 5¾ (6, 6¾) inches. Arrange five of the longer chains vertically between the patches as shown in the placement diagram and sew them in place, reserving the short chain and one of the long chains to sew between the patches along the side seam line once the seam has been stitched.

Pattern for yoke (1 square = 1")

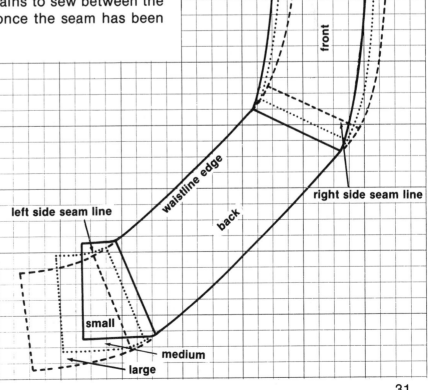

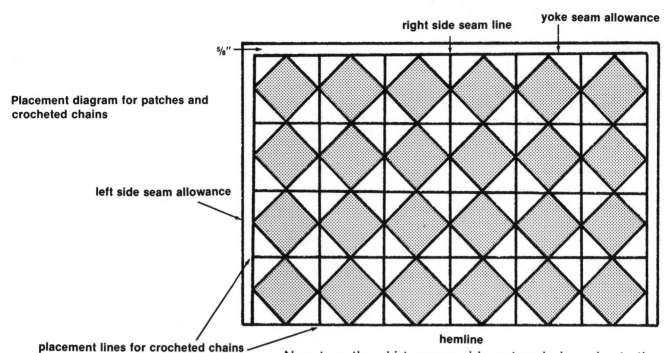

right side seam line

yoke seam allowance

⁵/₈"

Placement diagram for patches and crocheted chains

left side seam allowance

placement lines for crocheted chains

hemline

Now turn the skirt wrong side out and pin or baste the left side seam, taking care to align the rows of patches. Machine stitch the seam or backstitch by hand ⅝ inch in from the edge, leaving the bottom patch open for a slit. Turn the skirt right side out again, arrange the remaining long chain along the side seam and one side of the slit and sew it in place. Then stitch the short chain along the edge of the bottom patch on the opposite side of the slit. Cut away the excess seam allowances along the open portion of the side seam.

To finish the yoke, fold the long top (waistline) edge and the two short ends ¼ inch to the wrong side of the piece and pin. Topstitch along these three sides ⅛ inch in from the edge. Lap the end of the longer front section of the yoke 1 inch over the end of the shorter front section and pin the layers together. With the pieces right side out, pin the yoke to the skirt, lapping the bottom edge of the yoke over the top seam allowance of the skirt and aligning the left side seam and right side seam line markings of the skirt with the corresponding side seam line markings of the yoke. Then topstitch the yoke to the skirt ⅛ inch in from the bottom edge of the yoke. Finally, stitch the snap fasteners in place inside the yoke closure, and sew the frogs and buttons to the outside of the closure as shown in the photograph.

Patchwork designs, scenic wall hanging, and throw pillow, Chapter 3.

Home accessories you can make, Chapter 5.

His and her hangers and a pajama-bag pillow, Chapter 4.

Pussy cat pillow, doll, bank, and a child's very own toy box, Chapter 4.

Fashionable clothing and accessories for the entire family, Chapter 2.

WARM CAPE WITH A TOUCH OF FLAIR

All of us at some time or other want to own a cape for a touch of flair that's just a little different from anything else we have in our wardrobes. The cape shown here is warm and comfortable to wear over a pants suit, or a skirt or dress of any length—and its reversibility makes it doubly adaptable to whatever you'd like to wear it with. One size fits all, and while the cape in the photograph is black on one side and red on the other, it would be just as attractive in any other color or combination of colors that suits your own wardrobe best.

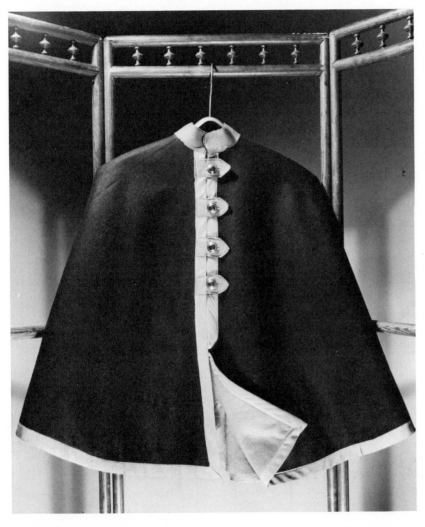

Materials
- 1¾ yds. 72"-wide black felt
- 1¾ yds. 72"-wide red felt
- 6 yds. 2"-wide red bias hem facing
- 4 detachable ¾" gold shank buttons with toggles
- black and red sewing thread

To Make

Trace the pattern pieces for the collar and tab. Cut two circles 54 inches in diameter for the cape, one from black and one from red, one black and one red collar(for these, folding the felt double, placing the pattern along the fold as indicated by the pattern markings, and cutting through two thicknesses), and four tabs each from red and black.

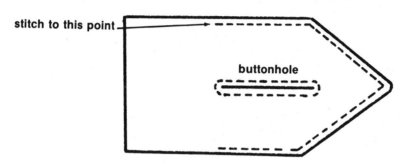

top edge

place on fold

neck edge

Collar pattern (actual size)

stitch to this point

buttonhole

Tab pattern (actual size)

To prepare the neckline and center front edges of the cape, first cut out a circle 4¼ inches in diameter from the center of both the black and the red circles. Then divide each large circle into six equal wedges and cut out one wedge, taking care to cut clean straight lines.

Pin the red and black cape pieces together, aligning all edges. Now pin the bias hem facing around the two center front edges and the bottom edge of the piece, mitering the tape at the corners. Then machine or hand stitch the tape in place with red thread, stitching as close as possible to the inner edge of the hem facing.

Place the red and black collar pieces together and topstitch around three sides, sewing ⅛ inch in from the edge and leaving the long neck seam line edge open. Then, keeping the black side of the cape and the red side of the collar facing out, insert the neckline edge of the cape ¼ inch into the open neck edge of the collar. Align the front edges of the cape and collar and ease the pieces to fit. Pin to hold and then topstitch through all layers close to the neckline edge of the collar.

To finish the tabs, place one red and one black tab piece together, and topstitch ⅛ inch in from the edge to the points indicated on the tab pattern (leave the back edge and 1 inch along each side open). Then make a 1-inch hand- or machine-worked buttonhole as shown on the pattern, and slit the buttonhole open. Complete the remaining three tabs in the same manner. Slip the open edges of the tabs around the right front edge of the cape, placing them with the red sides showing on the black side of the cape and spacing them as shown in the tab placement diagram. Pin and then topstitch the tabs in place. Mark the placement of the buttons at corresponding points on the left front edge of the cape. Then make a small hand- or machine-worked eyelet at each of these locations. Cut a small hole through the cape at the center of each eyelet, insert the button shanks through the holes and secure with toggles on the reverse side.

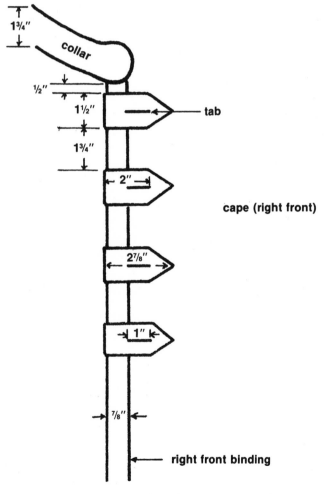

Placement diagram for tabs

3.
PATCHWORK

Patchwork, the technique of joining small pieces of material—often of different sizes, shapes, and colors—to create a larger whole, has been practiced for centuries in different forms and by different peoples around the world. But patchwork as we think of it today is really an art developed by the early American colonists. Having little opportunity to buy new fabrics, colonial women were forced to save every precious scrap of old cloth that wasn't too worn to be reused, and to resort to their rag bags to put together the yardage they needed to make warm bedcovers and hangings to protect windows and doors from cold winter drafts. By setting their creative imaginations to work at arranging their little bits of fabric in aesthetically pleasing ways, they transformed a necessary household task into a true folk art.

Today, patchwork is no longer made because it is necessary, but rather because it is attractive and fun to do. And many untraditional materials are now used, some of them—like the popular synthetic calicoes and percales—not even dreamed of when the traditions of American patchwork were being shaped. Felt, too, may not be traditional, but it is a perfect material for patchwork. Certainly patchwork with felt, as with any of the more commonly used woven materials, does involve joining many little pieces of different sizes, shapes, and colors; but felt has several advantages over woven fabrics. It is extremely easy to work with—to cut and to sew—even when intricate shapes are involved. More importantly, since the cut edges can't ravel, felt patches require no finishing and can be glued or bonded together edge to edge or joined in a variety of other interesting ways that are simply not practical with most woven patches. These characteristics make felt patchwork suitable for many kinds of projects that are quite different from those usually made with woven fabrics; and it is with this in mind that I offer the felt patchwork design ideas and projects in this chapter. I believe they will interest you and, hopefully, they will inspire creative thoughts of your own.

Edgings and Joinings

A simple, small rectangle of felt was the inspiration for the three interesting patchwork pieces shown here, each one finished and joined in a different way. One piece is assembled by edging and joining the individual rectangles with crochet stitches, another by edging the patches with embroidery and then sewing them together. For the third piece, the cut edges of the patches aren't finished at all, since they can't ravel, and the rectangles are simply arranged and glued in place on a backing. In the photographs, the patchwork pieces are shown in sample size, the crocheted and embroidered ones each made with twelve 3-inch by 5-inch cocoa brown patches, and the raw-edged piece made with eight 2-inch by 5-inch cocoa brown patches and eight 3-inch by 5-inch white ones. The choice of colors is, of course, up to you; and simply by adding rectangles horizontally (as was done to make the lamp shade cover project given in this chapter), vertically, or in both directions, or by eliminating rectangles (as was done to make the shopping bag project given in this chapter), you can make your own patchwork piece as large or as small as you need for a vest, tabard, poncho, bag, belt, or whatever other project you want to make. To correctly estimate how much material you will actually need for your project, however, it is always best to make a small sample with the particular edging and joining you plan to use. Remember, too, that these edgings and joinings can be used for any type of felt project regardless of whether it is something made of patchwork or something made of large plain sections of felt that need to be seamed together or edged.

RECTANGLE PATCHWORK STRIP WITH CROCHETED EDGES AND JOININGS

Crochet stitches make strong and attractive edges and join-ings for felt patchwork. The piece shown in the photograph was made by working single crochet stitches around the edges of the individual patches and then joining the patches, again with single crochet stitches. Felt patches can be pieced together with other crochet stitches as well, and directions are given for a shell stitch edging joined with chain stitches, and an openwork double crochet edging joined with chain stitches. Each of these edgings (as are all crocheted edgings on felt) is worked through a series of evenly spaced holes cut in the felt with a hole puncher.

Materials

- 12″ x 15″ piece of cocoa brown felt
- 2 oz. black medium-weight knitting yarn
- Size G crochet hook
- hole puncher

To Make

Cut the felt into twelve 3-inch by 5-inch rectangles. (To make a larger patchwork piece, use a bigger piece of felt and cut additional rectangles as needed.) Punch holes even-ly around the edges of each rectangle, spacing them ap-proximately ¼ inch apart and ¼ inch in from the edges of the felt. Then, following the diagram of the single crochet edg-ing, finish the individual rectangles by working one single crochet stitch through each hole along the edges and three single crochet in one hole to turn each of the corners. Arrange the rectangles as shown in the placement diagram for the crochet-edged patchwork, and join them on the right side of the piece with a row of single crochet stitches, working only through the back loops of the stitches as shown in the diagram for joining single crochet edges.

To make the shell stitch edging shown in the diagram, work three double crochets in one hole and one slip stitch in the next hole, then repeat the procedure around the edges of the piece. To join the individual rectangles, work one single crochet through the center stitch of two corresponding shells, chain one, and then continue this procedure until every pair of corresponding shells has been joined, as shown in the diagram of joining shell stitch edges.

To make the openwork double crochet edging shown in the diagram, work one double crochet in the first hole of the rectangle, chain one, work one double crochet in the next hole, chain one, and continue in this manner around the edges of the piece, except to work the double crochet, chain-one pattern stitch three times in each corner hole. To join the individual rectangles, work one single crochet in one of the double crochets, chain two, work one single crochet in the double crochet diagonally opposite, chain two, and continue in this manner, as shown in the diagram, until the pieces have been completely joined.

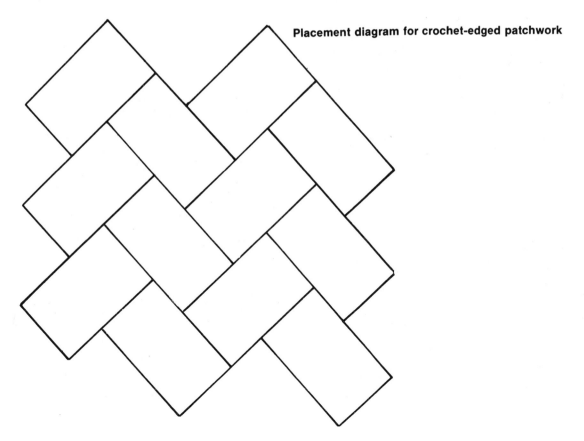

Placement diagram for crochet-edged patchwork

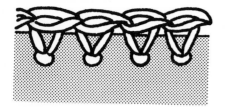

Single crochet edging

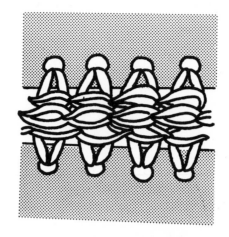

Joining single crochet edges

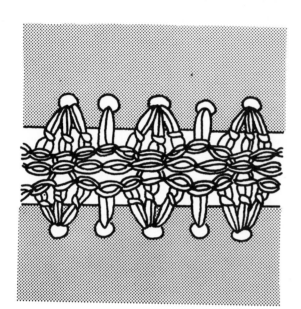

Joining shell edges

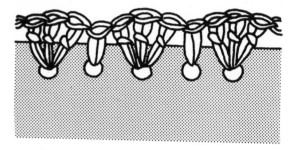

Crocheted shell edging

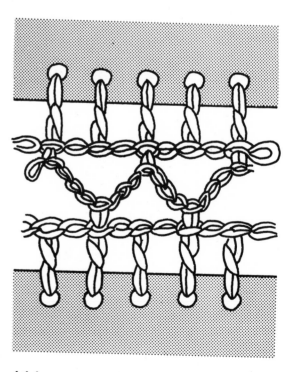

Joining openwork double crochet edges

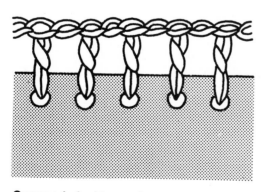

Openwork double crochet edging

LAMP SHADE COVER

This lamp shade cover is a perfect example of the fun of designing with felt patchwork, and shows just one of the many ways that patchwork rectangles edged and joined with crochet stitches can be used. The shade shown here is 11 inches high and approximately 45 inches in circumference, and to make the cover thirty-six cocoa brown rectangles were used. The same design can be adapted to suit any lamp shade you wish to cover simply by selecting a different color or combination of colors and by changing the number of patches used. Bear in mind, however, that for a lamp shade appreciably smaller than this one you should use smaller-sized patches, and for a much larger shade you should cut larger patches.

Materials
- ¼ yd. 72"-wide cocoa brown felt
- 4 oz. black medium-weight knitting yarn
- 1 lamp shade, 11" high and 45" in circumference
- double-faced adhesive tape
- Size G crochet hook
- hole puncher

To Make

Cut thirty-six 3-inch by 5-inch rectangles from the cocoa brown felt. Now punch holes around all the pieces and then edge and join them with single crochet as directed for the Rectangle Patchwork Strip with Crocheted Edgings and Joinings, adding patches to the sample strip horizontally. Join the two short ends of the piece with a row of single crochet, arranging the edges so the angled ends of the patches intermesh. Then slip the cover over the lamp shade, turn the extended ends of the patches to the inside of the shade along the top and bottom edges, and secure them with strips of double-faced adhesive tape.

RAW-EDGED RECTANGLE PATCHWORK STRIP

This easy-to-make patchwork strip takes advantage of the fact that the cut edges of felt don't require finishing. The rectangles are simply cut out and glued to a backing. Made here in cocoa brown and white, the striped pattern can be worked in any combination of colors and can be extended in any direction to make the yardage necessary for whatever felt project you have in mind.

Materials

- 18" x 28" piece of cocoa brown felt
- 10" x 12" piece of white felt
- white glue

To Make

From cocoa brown felt, cut eight 2-inch by 5-inch rectangles for the patches and one 18-inch square for the backing. Then cut eight 3-inch by 5-inch rectangles from white felt. (To make a larger patchwork piece, use bigger pieces of felt, and cut a larger backing square and additional patches as needed.) Arrange the rectangles on the backing as shown in the placement diagram for the raw-edged patchwork strip, alternating a stripe of four brown rectangles with a stripe of four white ones, and glue them in place. Then trim away the edges of the backing that extend beyond the rectangles.

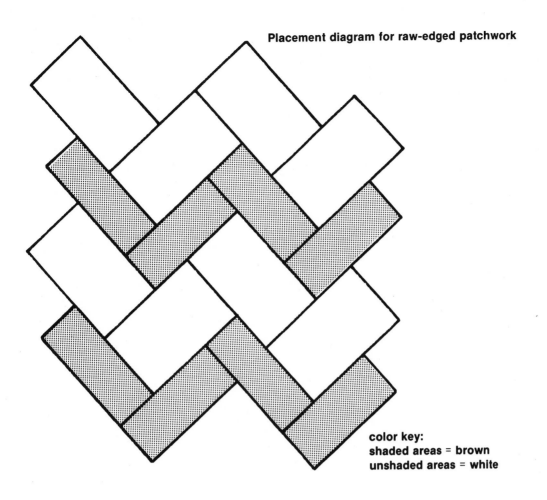

color key:
shaded areas = brown
unshaded areas = white

SHOPPING BAG

Trimmed with a design adapted from the Raw-Edged Rectangle Patchwork Strip, this roomy shopping bag is made from a soft vinyl in cocoa brown and measures 14 inches by 17 inches.

Materials

- 12" x 24" piece of cocoa brown felt
- 10" x 12" piece of white felt
- ⅝ yd. 36"-wide cocoa brown soft knit-backed vinyl
- ½ yd. lining material (optional)
- brown sewing thread
- white glue

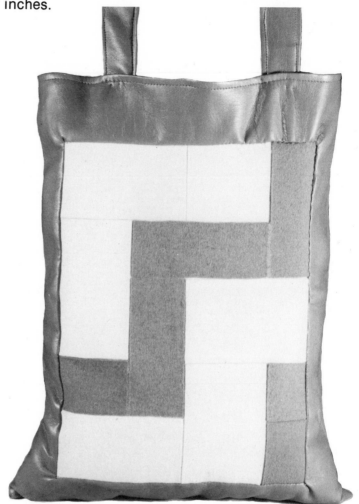

To Make

From cocoa brown felt, cut six 2-inch by 5-inch rectangles for the patches and one 10-inch by 13-inch rectangle for the patchwork backing. From white felt, cut six 3-inch by 5-inch patches. From the vinyl, cut two 15-inch by 18-inch rectangles for the front and back of the bag, and two 4-inch by 18-inch strips for the handles. If a lining is desired, cut two 15-inch by 18-inch rectangles from the lining material.

To make the patchwork trim for the front of the bag, arrange the brown and white patches on the felt backing rectangle as shown in the placement diagram for the patchwork trim, and glue them in place. Then trim away the edges of the four patches that extend beyond the edges of the backing.

Mark seam and cutting lines on the wrong side of one of the vinyl rectangles as shown in the marking and cutting diagram for the front of the shopping bag. Cut out the inner 8-inch by 11-inch rectangle along the cutting lines and discard it, then clip the corners diagonally, cutting just up to the seam line markings. With the pieces right sides together, stitch the remaining portion of the cut vinyl rectangle to the patchwork rectangle along the seam lines marked on the vinyl, taking care to align the edges of the seam allowances of the vinyl piece with the edges of the felt piece.

If a lining is desired, place one of the lining rectangles on the wrong side of the trimmed front of the bag and the other lining rectangle on the wrong side of the plain vinyl piece for the back of the bag. Then place the front and back sections of the bag together, wrong (or lining) sides out, and seam around three sides ½ inch in from the edges, leaving one of the short sides of the piece open. Turn the bag right side out and make the top hem by turning the raw top edge ½ inch to the wrong side and topstitching ¼ inch in from the folded edge.

To finish the bag, with the right side out, fold each long vinyl strap in half lengthwise, turn the long cut edges ½ inch to the inside of the piece, and then topstitch around all four sides ¼ inch in from the edge. Finally, sew the handles to the inside of the bag as shown in the photograph, positioning the outer edge of each strap 3 inches in from the side seam.

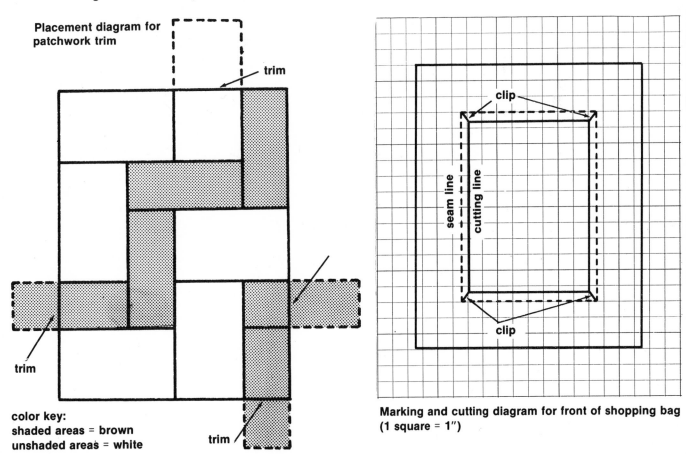

Placement diagram for patchwork trim

trim

trim

trim

trim

color key:
shaded areas = brown
unshaded areas = white

clip

seam line

cutting line

clip

Marking and cutting diagram for front of shopping bag (1 square = 1")

45

RECTANGLE PATCHWORK STRIP WITH EMBROIDERED EDGES AND JOININGS

Many different effects can be created by edging and joining felt patchwork with embroidery. The 3-inch by 5-inch rectangles shown in the photograph are edged with blanket stitch embroidery worked with knitting yarn, and then laced together with a simple whipstitch. There are a variety of other embroidery stitches that make attractive edgings, and two of them—the chain stitch and the Pekinese stitch—are also shown here. The stitches can be worked with embroidery floss instead of knitting yarn and, of course, the choice of colors for both felt and yarn is up to you. The simple whipstitch is recommended for joining all the embroidered edgings, but you can, if you prefer, substitute any of the crocheted joinings shown on pages 40 and 47.

Materials
- 12″ x 15″ piece of cocoa brown felt
- 2 oz. black medium-weight knitting yarn
- large-eyed embroidery needle
- hole puncher (optional)

46

To Make

From brown felt, cut twelve 3-inch by 5-inch rectangles. Work blanket stitches or, if you prefer, chain or Pekinese stitches around the edges of each rectangle as shown in the embroidery stitch diagrams. Stitch directly into the felt or, if you prefer, work the stitches through holes punched around the edges of the felt. Make blanket stitches (or the holes for them) approximately ¼ inch deep and space them ¼ inch apart; but work chain or Pekinese stitches only about ⅛ inch in from the edge of the felt. Then arrange the finished rectangles following the placement diagram for the crochet-edged patchwork on page 39, and lace them together with a whipstitch as shown in the diagram for the whipstitch joining.

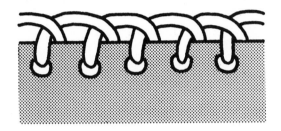

Blanket stitch edging

Chain stitch edging

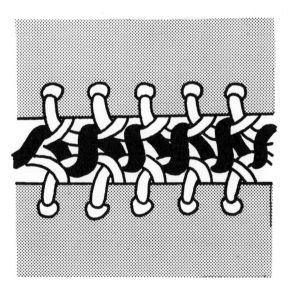

Whipstitch joining

Pekinese stitch edging

47

A Play of Geometrics

Squares, triangles, quarter circles, and other geometric forms provide the inspiration for this fascinating series of nine patchwork designs. Three basic pattern squares, each consisting of a few small geometric shapes arranged on a 6-inch-square felt background, serve as the building blocks for the larger designs. The individual squares shown here were made in ice-cream colors—vanilla, strawberry, and coffee for the small geometric pieces, and chocolate for the background—and the geometric shapes were applied to the background squares with bonding material. The choice of colors is your own, however, and you can affix the geometric pieces to the background with glue, or stitch them down with a needle and self-color thread, if you prefer. The larger designs, each one strikingly different from the next, measure 12 inches by 12 inches, and are created by taking four identical pattern squares and arranging them in different ways, turning them this way and that to achieve different effects in much the same way that rotating a kaleidoscope creates a variety of patterns from the same few bits of material. The designs can be enlarged or reduced in size to meet the requirements of your particular project—whether it be a handbag or a throw pillow, a quilt or a table cover, or just a trim for a patch pocket or a border—and they can be repeated in any direction to obtain the amount of yardage you need.

BASIC QUARTER CIRCLE AND ARC PATCH

Two arcs, a quarter circle, and a 6-inch square of felt, each in a different color, are all that you'll need to create this basic patchwork square. The unusual patchwork designs that follow are made by stitching four of these individual squares together in varying arrangements. A single 6-inch square can be cut from scraps of felt; the 12-inch multiple-square designs require slightly larger pieces.

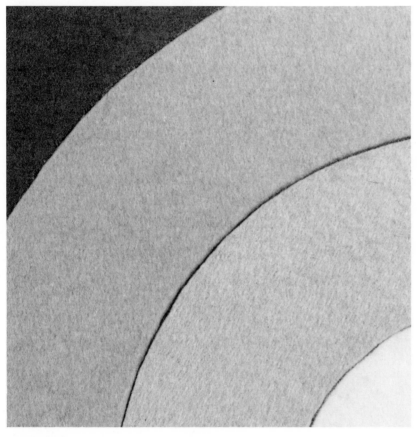

Materials
- scraps of chocolate, vanilla, strawberry, and coffee felt
- 6" square of fusible bonding material

color key:
v = vanilla
ch = chocolate
s = strawberry
c = coffee

To Make

Trace the pattern for the quarter circle and arc patch and enlarge it to full size (instructions for enlarging are given in Chapter 8). From chocolate felt, cut a 6-inch square for the backing; cut a quarter circle from vanilla, a small arc from coffee, and a large arc from strawberry, following the outlines of the pattern pieces; then cut one of each of these three shapes from the bonding material.

Place the three geometric felt shapes on top of the appropriate pieces of bonding material, arrange them on the square of chocolate felt as shown on the pattern, and affix them to the backing with an iron as directed on the package of bonding material.

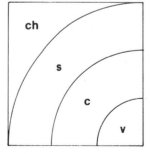

Pattern for quarter circle and arc patch (¼ actual size)

49

THREE QUARTER CIRCLE AND ARC PATCHWORK DESIGNS

By simply juggling and rearranging the placement of four identical quarter circle and arc patches, any number of different designs can be created. Three interesting four-patch design arrangements are shown here, along with a pattern for each one, and those of you who enjoy working jigsaw puzzles will find it a real challenge to see how many additional designs you can make with the same four individual squares. The four component patches for each design are cut and assembled separately, and then stitched together with a whipstitch.

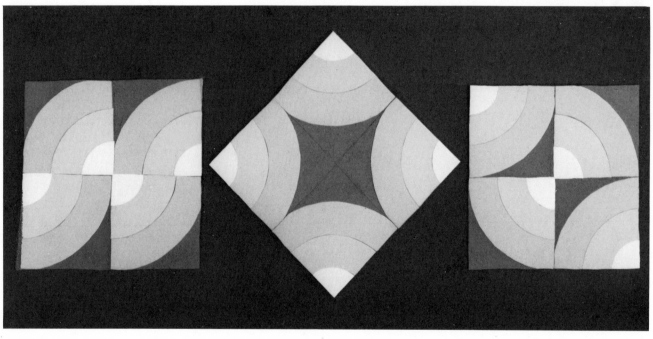

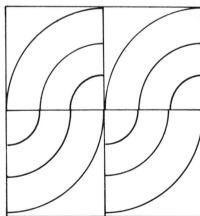

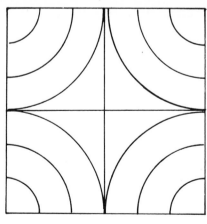

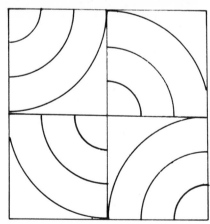

Quarter circle and arc design No. 1   Quarter circle and arc design No. 2   Quarter circle and arc design No. 3

FRINGED PILLOW

A patchwork design made with four quarter circle and arc patches is the focal point of this stunning contemporary pillow. Measuring 22 inches square, the pillow is fringed with yarn on the back and around the edges of the patchwork square.

Materials
- 24" x 30" piece of chocolate felt
- scraps of vanilla, coffee, and orange felt
- 4 4 oz. skeins chocolate medium-weight knitting yarn
- 4 4 oz. skeins orange medium-weight knitting yarn
- ¾ yd. 40"-wide 3½-mesh-per-inch rug canvas
- 12" square of fusible bonding material
- 22" square foam pillow form
- brown sewing thread
- latch hook

To Make
Trace the pattern for the Basic Quarter Circle and Arc Patch given in this chapter, and enlarge it to full size (instructions for enlarging are given in Chapter 8). From chocolate felt, cut one 24-inch square for the front of the pillow, and four 6-inch squares as backing for the circle and arc patches; then cut four quarter-circle pieces from vanilla, four small arcs from coffee, and four large arcs from orange, following the outlines of the patch patterns. Cut a piece of bonding material in the same shape as each of the geometric felt pieces. Finally, from the rug canvas, cut one 16-inch square for the front of the pillow and one 24-inch square for the back of the pillow.

Make four quarter circle and arc patches following the directions for the Basic Quarter Circle and Arc Patch given in this chapter. Then arrange the patches following the pattern for Quarter Circle and Arc Design No. 2 (see page 50), and sew them together from the wrong side with a whipstitch, taking care that the stitches do not show on the right side of the work.

Center the finished patchwork piece on the 16-inch square of rug canvas and whipstitch it in place around the edges. Now cut a number of 3-inch strands of chocolate and orange yarn, and knot two strands (one of each color) into each mesh of the canvas with the latch hook, leaving 1 inch of the canvas unfringed along each edge for hemming. Turn the hem allowance to the wrong side of the canvas and whipstitch it in place, mitering the corners to eliminate bulk. Then center the fringed patchwork piece right side up on the chocolate felt pillow front, and whipstitch it in place around the edges.

To make the back of the pillow, fringe the entire 24-inch square of rug canvas, again knotting two strands of yarn into each mesh of the canvas with the latch hook and leaving a 1-inch hem allowance unfringed around the edges. Now place the patchwork-trimmed pillow front and the fringed pillow back together, wrong sides out, and seam 1 inch in from the edge around three sides of the work. Trim the seam allowances to ½ inch, and turn the pillow cover right side out. Then insert the foam pillow form and seam the open side of the piece. Finally, trim the ends of the fringes evenly where necessary.

BASIC TRIANGLE PATCH

Four strawberry and coffee triangles, and one four-sided vanilla shape were mounted on a 6-inch square of chocolate felt to make this interesting geometric patch, which is the source of inspiration for the three larger patchwork designs that follow. Like the other geometric patches, this one requires only a few scraps of felt.

Materials
- scraps of chocolate, vanilla, strawberry, and coffee felt
- 6″ square of fusible bonding material

color key:
v = vanilla
ch = chocolate
s = strawberry
c = coffee

To Make

Trace the pattern for the triangle patch, and enlarge it to full size (instructions for enlarging are given Chapter 8).

From chocolate felt, cut a 6-inch square for the backing. Cut one four-sided shape from vanilla felt, two large triangles from strawberry felt, and two small triangles from coffee felt, following the outlines of the pattern pieces; then cut a piece of bonding material in the same shape as each of the geometric pieces.

Place the felt shapes on top of the appropriate pieces of bonding material, arrange them on the square of chocolate felt as shown on the pattern, and iron them to the backing as directed on the package of bonding material.

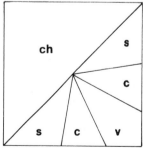

**Pattern for triangle patch
(¼ actual size)**

THREE TRIANGLE PATCHWORK DESIGNS

The three patchwork designs shown here, each very different in its own way, are the result of a little playing around with the placement of four of the small triangle patches. The arrangement of squares for each design is illustrated in the diagrams, and you can create many more patterns yourself simply by rearranging the four component squares in other ways.

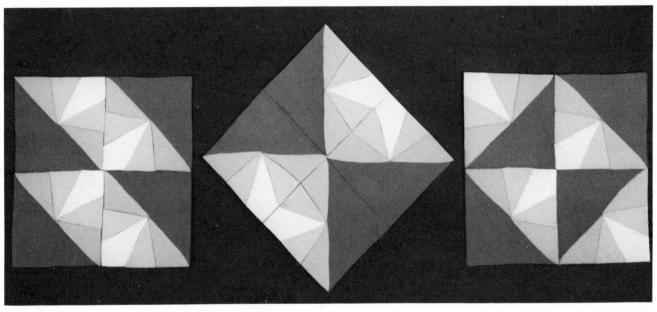

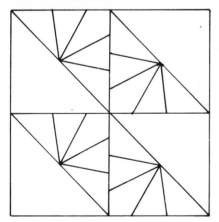

Triangle design No. 1

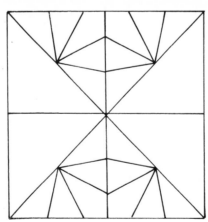

Triangle design No. 2

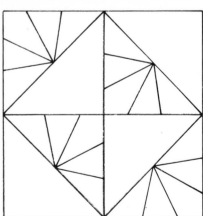

Triangle design No. 3

BASIC RIGHT-ANGLE PATCH

A small vanilla square and two right-angle pieces, in coffee and strawberry, are mounted on a 6-inch chocolate square to create the basic pattern for the three larger geometric patchwork designs that follow.

Materials

- scraps of chocolate, vanilla, strawberry, and coffee felt
- 6″ square of fusible bonding material

color key:
v = vanilla
ch = chocolate
s = strawberry
c = coffee

To Make

Trace the pattern for the right-angle patch, and enlarge it to full size (instructions for enlarging are given in Chapter 8).

From chocolate felt, cut a 6-inch square for the backing. Cut one small right-angle piece from coffee felt and one large right-angle piece from strawberry felt, following the outlines of the pattern pieces; then cut a piece of bonding material in the same shape as each of the geometric pieces.

Place the felt shapes on top of the appropriate pieces of bonding material, arrange them on the square of chocolate felt as shown on the pattern, and affix them to the backing with an iron as directed on the package of bonding material.

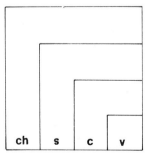

Pattern for right-angle patch (¼ actual size)

THREE RIGHT-ANGLE PATCHWORK DESIGNS

Three different ways to arrange the four small right-angle patches are shown in this photograph and in the design diagrams that follow. They illustrate just a few of the many possible designs that can be created with these very simple patches, and you may find it great fun to see how many additional patterns you can come up with yourself.

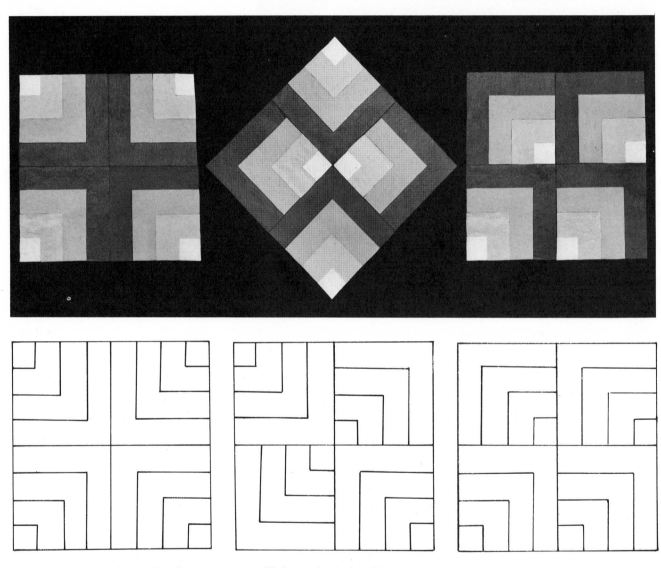

Right-angle design No. 1   Right-angle design No. 2   Right-angle design No. 3

Two Patchwork Projects

Now that you've learned how to finish and join felt pieces, and how to play with little geometric shapes to create larger patchwork designs, you may be interested in making a completely different patchwork project from start to finish. Full instructions are given here for a throw pillow and a wall hanging, and while both are very unusual pieces, each is quite simple to make. The design for the pillow is based on the idea of arranging many identically shaped geometric patches—in this case a "doughnut" shape—on a piece of background fabric to create a pattern. The highly stylized scenic wall hanging, on the other hand, is made from pieces of many different geometric shapes that are fitted together in jigsaw-puzzle fashion to create the overall composition. Once you've made one or both of these projects, you'll find it easy to use the ideas on which they are based as a takeoff point for original designs of your own—perhaps a pillow made with a series of squares or rectangles (or a combination of both) in whatever profusion of colors you choose, spread onto a background; or a scene traced from a painting or photograph and then transformed into many small felt pieces of different shapes that fit together to form a patchwork picture.

THROW PILLOW

Seventy-four coffee and beige doughnut shapes, arranged diagonally in alternate-color stripes on a square of hot pink felt, form the design for this throw pillow, which measures 20 inches square, including the ruffled edges.

Materials

- ½ yd. 72"-wide hot pink felt
- ¼ yd. 72"-wide coffee felt
- ¼ yd. 72"-wide beige felt
- 1½ lbs. polyester fiberfill stuffing
- coffee, beige, and hot pink sewing thread

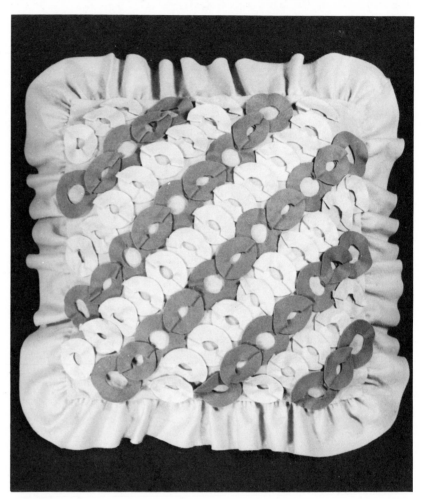

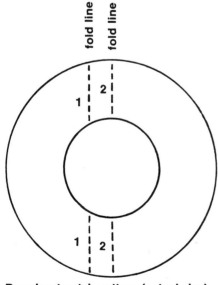

Doughnut patch pattern (actual size)

To Make

Trace the pattern for the doughnut patch. Cut thirty-five doughnut-shaped patches from coffee felt and thirty-nine patches from beige felt, following the outlines of the pattern; and from hot pink, cut two 15-inch squares for the pillow and four 2¾-inch by 30-inch strips for the ruffled edging.

Using the fold lines marked on the doughnut patch pattern as a guide, fold a ¼-inch tuck on two opposite sides of each beige doughnut piece, then stitch the tucks down with self-color thread so they lie flat. Repeat this procedure with fifteen of the coffee doughnut pieces.

Arrange all of the doughnut patches on one of the 15-inch pink felt squares as shown in Placement Diagram (A) and sew them in place, overlapping the edges as shown in Placement Diagrams (B) and (C). To make the ruffle, gather one long edge of each 30-inch pink strip with sewing thread, drawing up the thread until the piece measures 15 inches and adjusting the gathers evenly. Then sew the gathered strips around the doughnut-trimmed pillow square, placing them ¼ inch under the edges and stitching the short ends together at the corners. Finally, place the two pink squares together, right sides out, and topstitch along three sides. Stuff the pillow firmly, and then sew the edges together along the remaining side.

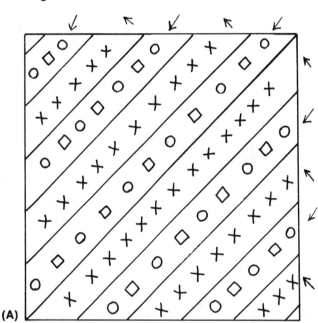

(A)

Placement diagrams for doughnut patches. Arrange patches on background square as in diagram (A), positioning fold lines in direction indicated by arrows. Overlap edges of beige patches as in diagram (B), and edges of coffee patches as in diagram (C)

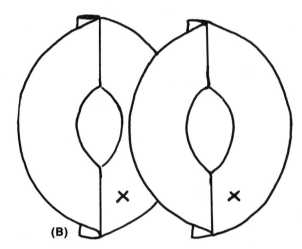

(B)

patch placement key:
o = unfolded coffee patch
□ = folded coffee patch
X = folded beige patch

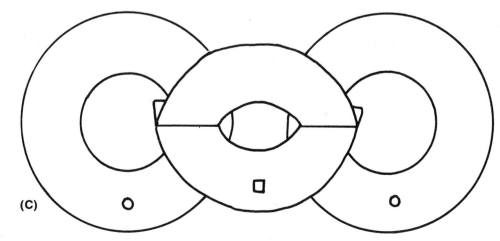

(C)

59

SCENIC WALL HANGING

This delightful wall hanging, measuring 25 inches by 29 inches, is made from little more than scraps of felt, in a rainbow of colors, mounted on a large felt rectangle. Ovals, squares, triangles, rectangles, and other geometric and free-form shapes are transformed into houses, trees, river, sky, and all the other component parts of this charming village scene.

Materials

- ¾ yd. 72"-wide brown felt
- scraps of white, beige, hot pink, baby blue, aqua, pearl grey, coffee, apricot, jade green, kelly green, and black felt
- 1 lightweight curtain rod
- brown sewing thread
- white glue

To Make

Enlarge the pattern for the village scene to full size (instructions for enlarging are given in Chapter 8). From brown felt, cut a 25-inch by 30½-inch rectangle as a backing for the hanging. Then, using the color key as a guide, mark the outline of all the individual pieces of the scene on felt scraps of the appropriate color, and cut out the pieces. Note that each doorknob should be cut from the same color felt as the wall on which the particular door is hung; and all window panes are made by cutting a piece of apricot felt in the same shape as each of the window frames.

Trim out the panes from all the window frame pieces and glue the frames to the corresponding apricot pieces for the panes. Then arrange all the pieces of the scene on the brown felt backing, leaving a 1½-inch border at the bottom and sides and a 3-inch border at the top, and glue them in place. Finish the hanging by making a casing for the rod across the top border of the piece. To do this, fold the top edge 1½ inches to the wrong side of the piece and seam the layers together across the bottom of the casing.

Color key:
A = white   G = coffee
B = beige   H = apricot
C = hot pink   I = jade
D = baby blue   J = kelly green
E = aqua   K = black
F = pearl gray   L = brown

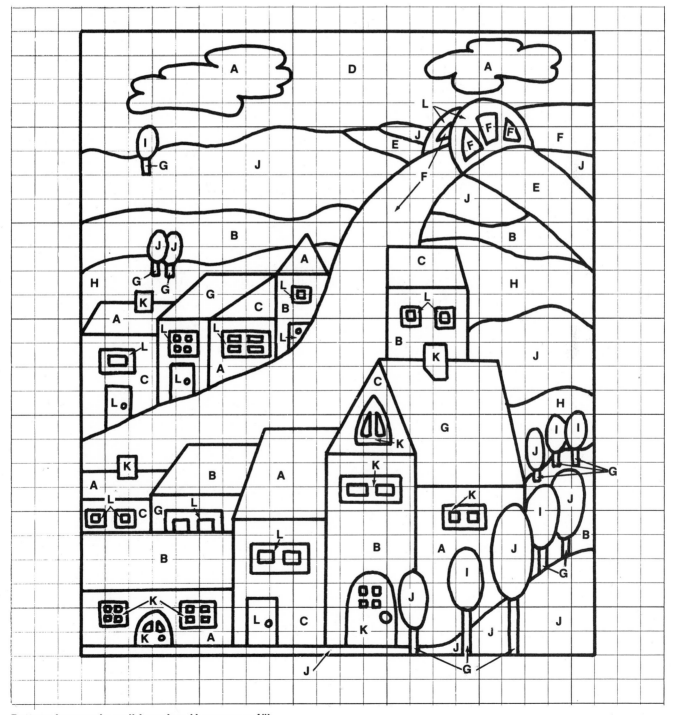

Pattern for scenic wall hanging (1 square = 1″)

4. TOYS

Bank

Rubio the Clown—A Pajama Bag

Ducky Lucky—A Silly Puppet

Portrait of a Bashful Little Bear

Jigsaw Puzzle

Valerie—Someone's Favorite Doll

Pussy Cat Pillow

Long Green Crocodile—Another Puppet

Your Name Shapes a Special Pillow

His and Her Clothes Hangers

Funny Little Men Ride on a Choo-Choo

Big Chest for Storing Little Toys

So many of us have experienced the simple pleasure of standing outside a toy store in the company of a young child, and watching the glow on the face of the little one as he (or she) stared entranced at the sight of all the wonderful playthings inside the store window. Often we've been tempted to buy all the things that our young and wide-eyed companion has practically finger-handled through the glass, and once in a while—although certainly not as often as we might like to—most of us have actually gone inside and bought one of them. But toys are expensive, and we've usually had to resist the temptation to enter the store simply because we couldn't afford to buy anything at the moment.

You won't have to resist the temptation to enter my own little felt Toy Shop, however, because all the toys on display here are not only delightful, they are affordable as well. By and large they require little more than a small amount of felt and stuffing material, some inexpensive and readily available trimmings, and a little patience on your part to study the easy-to-follow instructions for making them, in return for which you will be able to make some of the little people you know very happy indeed. And I have no doubt that they will love these toys as much as any of the ones they've seen in store windows, having had a bit of a problem myself trying to keep the design samples for this book from mysteriously disappearing as soon as they were finished. Young visitors to my house have vied with one another for the toys, and have even had minor skirmishes over who would play with the duck puppet or the jigsaw puzzle, and who would inherit the choo-choo train or the toy chest once I no longer needed them. One little fellow, in fact, even deposited a few of his own pennies in the felt bank to insure that this particular toy would eventually belong to him!

BANK

Looking something like the real bank down the block, this miniature model is 8 inches long, 4 inches wide, and 4 inches tall—just the right size to stand on top of a small table or low chest within easy reach of the young penny depositor.

Materials

- ¼ yd. 72"-wide white felt
- scraps of yellow, black, green, red, and blue felt
- small amount of black medium-weight knitting yarn
- small amount of black embroidery thread
- 1 empty half-gallon milk carton
- 1 3½" wide x 4½" long x ¾" deep cardboard gift box
- 4" square of cardboard
- 2 sheets of typing paper
- 4 ½"-in-diameter white Velcro fastener circles
- masking tape
- white glue
- black marking pen
- utility knife

To Make

Trace the pattern for the bank facade applique trim. From white felt, cut one 8½-inch by 17-inch rectangle and two 4-inch squares to cover the milk carton and one 6½-inch by 7½-inch rectangle to cover the gift box. Then, using the color key as a guide, mark the outline of the various pieces for the bank facade appliqué trim on felt scraps of the appropriate color, and cut out the pieces.

Rinse and dry the milk carton thoroughly, then cut off the spout (the height of the remaining portion of the carton should be approximately 8 inches). Cover the open top of the carton with the cardboard square, trimming the cardboard to fit and taping it in place securely with masking tape. Then reinforce the entire carton so it will hold its shape by wrapping strips of masking tape around it in both lengthwise directions. Cut the typing paper to fit and glue it around the top, bottom and sides of the carton. Now glue the large white felt rectangle around the sides of the carton, and glue the 4-inch squares to the ends, trimming the felt as necessary. Allow the glue to dry thoroughly and then cut a 2-inch by 3-inch opening in the center of one long side of the carton (this side will be the "roof" of the bank).

To make a lid for the roof of the bank, cut a 2-inch by 3-inch opening in the bottom of the gift box. Then close the box and tape it closed with masking tape. Now glue the small white felt rectangle around the top and sides of the box, mitering the corners, and turn the excess felt under the bottom of the box and glue it down. Make the coin deposit slot by cutting a ⅛-inch by 2-inch slit lengthwise down the center of the top of the box. Finally, to make the lid easily removable when bank withdrawals are necessary, separate the four Velcro circles and glue one layer of them to the bottom of the box at the corners. Then center the box over the hole cut in the roof of the bank, glue the other layer of Velcro circles in corresponding places on the bank, and press the box in place.

Finish the appliqué trim for the bank facade by embroidering window pulls on the window shades and the word "BANK" on the top of the door as shown on the pattern, and marking dots and hands on the face of the clock with marking pen. Glue the appliqué pieces in place on the front of the bank as shown on the pattern. Then outline the door and the two windows, as well as the four edges of the bank facade, with black yarn, and glue the yarn in place.

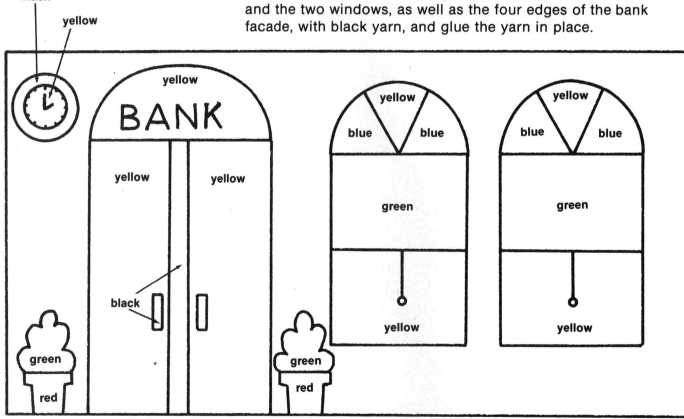

Pattern for bank facade appliqué trim (actual size)

RUBIO THE CLOWN – A PAJAMA BAG

Rubio, a funny clown, takes his rest by night but works double duty in the daytime, when he serves as a pajama bag and, once filled, as a soft pillow for show or for leaning against while stretched out watching TV.

Materials

- ½ yd. 72"-wide white felt
- 10" x 12" piece of red felt
- 10" x 12" piece of light blue felt
- 7" x 14" piece of yellow felt
- scraps of royal blue and black felt
- 2 oz. red medium-weight knitting yarn
- white sewing thread
- white glue

To Make

Trace the pattern for the clown and enlarge it to full size (instructions for enlarging are given in Chapter 8). From white felt, cut two clown pieces, following the outline of the pattern. Then, using the color key as a guide, mark the outlines of the various appliqué pieces for the hat and facial features on felt of the appropriate color, and cut out the pieces.

Cut horizontally across one of the large white felt clown pieces along the broken line marked on the pattern, and stay stitch each piece close to the cut edge. Now place the two cut pieces together with the uncut clown piece, align the edges, and then stitch the pieces together around the entire edge, sewing ⅛ inch in from the edge.

To finish the clown, glue all the appliqué pieces in place as shown on the pattern. From red yarn, make two 5-inch pompons for the hair, and one 2-inch pompon to trim the top of the hat, and sew these in place as shown in the photograph.

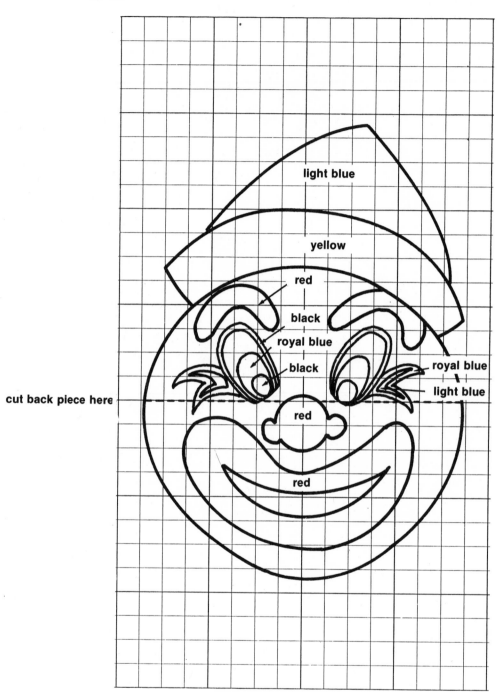

light blue

yellow

red

black

royal blue

black

royal blue

light blue

cut back piece here

red

red

Pattern for Rubio the clown (1 square = 1")

DUCKY LUCKY—A SILLY PUPPET

Funny little eyes and a bright yellow curl at the top of his head make Lucky look awfully silly, and when you manipulate him, he'll practically quack back at you with his oversized orange beak.

Materials

- 12″ x 24″ piece of yellow felt
- scraps of orange felt
- small amount of yellow medium-weight knitting yarn
- small amount of polyester fiberfill stuffing
- 2 ½″ eye buttons
- yellow sewing thread
- orange dressmaker's carbon paper
- tracing wheel

To Make

Enlarge the pattern pieces for the duck puppet to full size (instructions for enlarging are given in Chapter 8). From yellow felt, cut two main pieces for the front and back of the puppet, and, from orange, two pieces each for the top and bottom of the beak. With dressmaker's carbon paper transfer the placement lines for the beak and the stitching lines marked on the wings to one piece of the felt (this piece will be the front of the puppet).

Place the two pieces for the top of the back together and topstitch around all sides ⅛ inch in from the edge. Stitch together the two pieces for the bottom of the beak in the same manner. Then sew the beak pieces in place along the placement lines marked on the front of the puppet. Tack the ends of the beak pieces together, and then sew on the eyes.

Now place the front and back of the puppet together, right sides out, and topstitch ⅛ inch in from the edge, leaving the bottom open. Then lightly stuff the sections of the wings marked "S" on the pattern, and topstitch through all layers along the stitching lines marked on the wings. Finish the puppet by tacking a few loops of yarn to the top of the head as shown in the photograph.

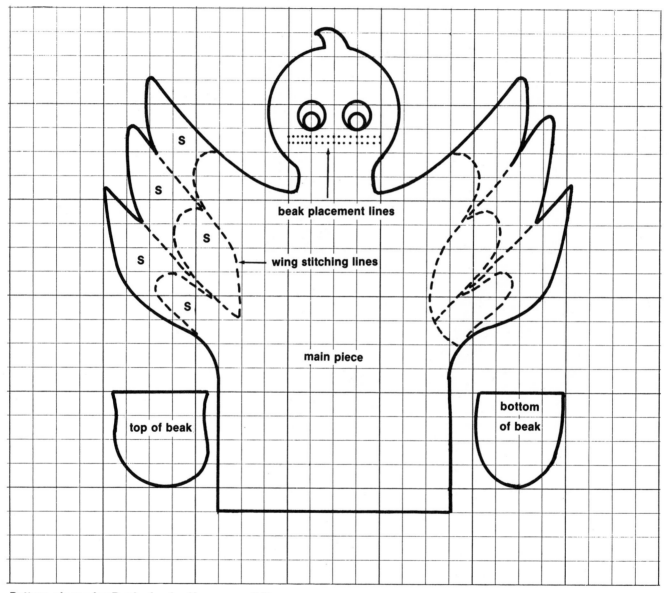

Pattern pieces for Ducky Lucky (1 square = ½″)

PORTRAIT OF A BASHFUL
LITTLE BEAR

Measuring 16 inches by 24 inches, the felt-framed portrait of this cute little fellow shows him sucking his thumb as he carries a flower for someone he especially likes.

Materials
- 20" x 30" piece of white felt
- 12" x 28" piece of brown felt
- 12" x 26" piece of royal blue felt
- 10" x 20" piece of green felt
- 6" x 10" piece of beige felt
- scraps of red, yellow, and black felt
- 16" x 24" piece of medium-weight cardboard
- double-faced adhesive tape
- white glue
- pinking shears

To Make
Enlarge the patterns for the portrait and the flower to full size (instructions for enlarging are given in Chapter 8).

From white felt, cut a 19-inch by 27-inch piece for the background of the portrait; from royal blue, two 3-inch by 18-inch strips and two 3-inch by 26-inch strips for the frame; then, using the color key as a guide, mark the outline of all the various pieces of the portrait on felt of the appropriate color, marking the legs and one arm separately as shown on the pattern, and cut out the pieces.

Cover the cardboard with the piece of white felt, turning under the extended 1½-inch edges on all sides and securing them to the back of the cardboard with double-faced tape. Now glue all the pieces of the portrait in place on the background, layering them as necessary and arranging the flower in the bear's outstretched hand as shown in the photograph. Finally, cut one long edge of each of the royal blue strips for the frame with a pinking shears. Arrange the strips to form a 1-inch frame around the portrait, with the pinked edges forming the inner edges of the frame, and glue them in place. Then turn the extended edges of the strips to the back of the piece and secure them with double-faced tape.

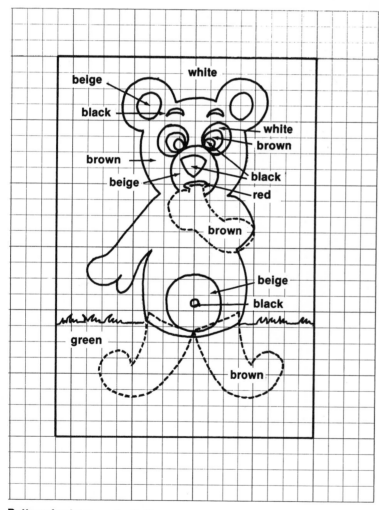

Pattern for bear portrait (1 square = 1")

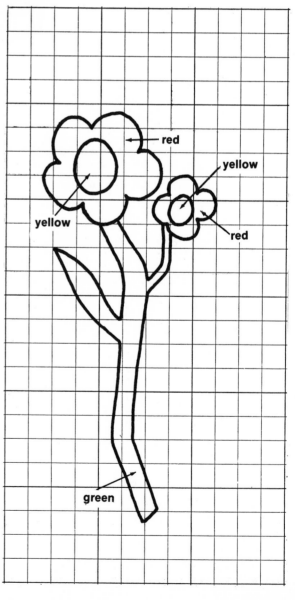

Flower pattern (1 square = ½")

JIGSAW PUZZLE

Young and old, we all enjoy the challenge of working a jigsaw puzzle. While the more experienced among us can often work with as many as several hundred pieces, youngsters are happier with just a few large cutouts. The familiar farm scene shown here is just about right for three- to six-year-olds. It consists of twenty-five 2½-inch-square felt pieces that fit easily together, and it is made from nothing more than a few small pieces of felt and a piece of cardboard.

Materials
- 10" by 12" piece of dark green felt
- 6" x 12" piece of light blue felt
- 5" x 8" piece of yellow felt
- 6" x 8" piece of light green felt
- 5" x 6" piece of gray felt
- 5" x 9" piece of white felt
- scraps of red, black, orange, brown, and royal blue felt
- 12½" square of medium-weight cardboard
- white glue
- black marking pen
- sharp scissors

To Make
Enlarge the pattern for the jigsaw puzzle to full size (instructions for enlarging are given in Chapter 8). Using the color key as a guide, mark the outline of the various pattern pieces of the jigsaw puzzle on felt of the appropriate color, and cut out the pieces.

Glue the felt pieces to the cardboard backing as shown on the pattern, layering them as necessary. With the black marking pen, draw in the fine lines on the cow's face and legs, the duck's eye, and the door for the barn, following the pattern. Finally, cut the finished piece into 2½-inch squares. If desired, make a 1-inch cardboard frame into which the pieces can be set as the puzzle is worked, and cover the frame with strips of black felt.

color key:

A = black	G = red
B = dark green	H = royal blue
C = gray	I = white
D = light blue	J = yellow
E = light green	K = brown
F = orange	L = black marking pen

Pattern for jigsaw puzzle (1 square = ½")

VALERIE—
SOMEONE'S FAVORITE DOLL

With her long blond pigtails and a look of starry wonder in her eyes, Valerie is a little cutie pie. She is 25 inches tall and her clothes are removable, and if you're ambitious you can make many other outfits for her to wear from small pieces of leftover material in your scrap bag.

Materials

- 1/3 yd. 72"-wide flesh-tone felt
- 1/3 yd. 72"-wide medium green felt
- ¼ yd. 72"-wide white felt
- scraps of blue, red, and black felt
- 2 yds. 1"-wide white gathered eyelet trim
- 2 oz. yellow medium-weight knitting yarn
- 3" piece of narrow black elastic
- ½ lb. polyester fiberfill stuffing
- 3 small snap fasteners
- pink, white, green, and black sewing thread
- elastic thread
- red crayon
- 8" square of cardboard
- white glue

To Make

Enlarge the pattern pieces for Valerie and her clothes to full size (instructions for enlarging are given in Chapter 8), then trace the patterns for Valerie's facial features. For the doll, from the flesh-tone felt, cut two body pieces, four arms, and a circle ¾ inch in diameter for the nose; then cut one mouth and the various pieces for two eyes and eyelashes from scraps of felt in the colors indicated on the patterns; for the clothes and accessories, from white felt cut two pantaloon pieces, two blouse pieces, and two sleeves; from green, one 12-inch by 40-inch piece for the skirt, one 1-inch by 32-inch strip for the waistband, two ½-inch by 12-inch strips for pigtail bows, and one ¼-inch by 8-inch strip for a choker necklace; and for the shoes, from black cut two uppers, two soles, and two side pieces.

To make Valerie, sew the two body pieces together, right sides out, with a whipstitch, working from the bottom of the feet toward the head and stuffing as you go (be careful not to overstuff). As you reach the ankle, knee, and hip joints, and the waist (indicated on the pattern by broken-line markings), stitch across the piece through all layers. Now stitch together the pieces for each arm, stuffing as you sew, and whipstitch the arms to the body. Then finish the face by glueing the mouth and the pieces for the eyes and lashes in place as shown on the patterns. Make a nose by running a gathering stitch around the edge of the ¾-inch flesh-tone circle, stuffing the piece, and drawing up the gathering thread tightly. Stitch the nose in place on the face.

Pattern pieces for Valerie and her clothes (1 square = 1″)

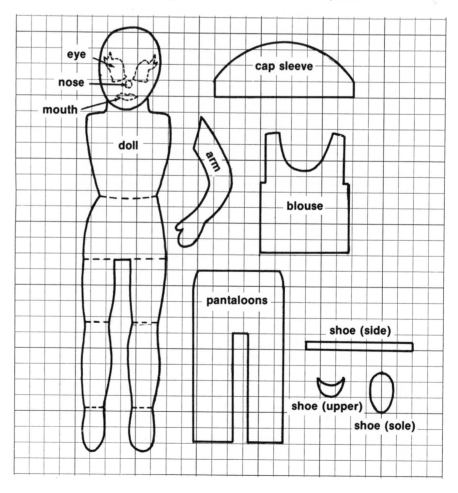

To make Valerie's wig, wind the yellow yarn around the 8-inch cardboard square, wrapping for 5½ inches across the cardboard. Make the center part by sewing a 5½-inch row of chain stitches with the yarn along one edge of the cardboard, and then cut the yarn along the opposite edge of the cardboard. Center the wig on Valerie's head and tack it in place. Gather the yarn ends into two pigtails and tie each with a bow made from one of the narrow 12-inch strips of green felt.

To make Valerie's clothes, sew together the two pantaloon pieces, right sides out, with a whipstitch. Run a gathering stitch around the waist with elastic thread, drawing up the thread for a good fit. Then stitch two rows of eyelet trim around the bottom of each leg.

Place the two blouse pieces together, right sides out, and stitch the shoulder and side seams by whipping the edges together. Make a back opening by slitting one of the blouse pieces lengthwise down the center. Stitch the underarm seam of each sleeve, then run a gathering stitch around each sleeve cap and draw up the thread until the sleeve cap fits the armhole. Insert the sleeves in the armholes of the blouse and sew them in place. Now gather the hem edge of each sleeve to fit around the doll's arm, and stitch two rows of eyelet trim around the edge. Finish the blouse by stitching two rows of eyelet around the neckline, and then sew the snap fasteners in place along the back opening.

To make the skirt, run a gathering stitch along one of the 40-inch edges of the large green felt rectangle, and draw up the thread until the piece fits comfortably around the doll's waist. Lap one long edge of the waistband ¼ inch over the gathered edge of the skirt, allowing the excess length of the waistband to extend equally beyond the ends of the skirt piece, and then topstitch the band to the skirt. To finish, turn the skirt wrong side out and stitch the center back seam, sewing ¼ inch in from the edge and leaving a 2-inch opening at the top.

To make the shoes, whipstitch one long edge of the side pieces around the edges of the soles, starting and ending at the center back. If the side pieces are too long, trim off the excess, and then stitch the short ends together for a center back seam. Now whipstitch the uppers to the top edges of the side pieces at the front of the shoes. Cut the strip of black elastic into two 1½-inch pieces, and sew one piece across the instep of each shoe.

Finally, dress Valerie in her clothes and shoes, and place the narrow green strip for the choker around her neck, tacking the two ends together at the back.

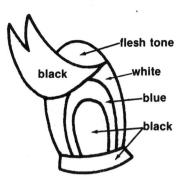

Eye pattern (actual size)

Mouth pattern (actual size)

PUSSY CAT PILLOW

Sweet and friendly, and cuddly soft, too, this little pussy cat pillow will be as happy to find a home in some child's room as the child will be to have him. He measures about 10 inches by 14 inches and is very easy to make.

Materials

- 1/3 yd. 72"-wide orange felt
- 2 oz. black medium-weight knitting yarn
- 2 oz. yellow medium-weight knitting yarn
- small amount of green medium-weight knitting yarn
- ½ lb. polyester fiberfill stuffing
- orange sewing thread
- large-eyed embroidery needle
- white dressmaker's carbon paper
- tracing wheel

To Make

Enlarge the pattern for the pillow to full size (instructions for enlarging are given in Chapter 8). Cut two cat pieces from the orange felt, and transfer all the pattern markings to one of the pieces with a tracing wheel and dressmaker's carbon paper (instructions for transferring pattern markings are also given in Chapter 8).

Now embroider the marked piece, working all lines in black with an outline stitch. Fill in the forehead blaze, the ears, the tip of the tail, and the paws with a long-and-short satin stitch in yellow. Use a satin stitch in green for the collar and the irises of the eyes; and work a satin stitch in black for the nose, the mouth, and the pupils of the eyes.

To finish the pillow, place the two felt pieces together, right sides out, and topstitch ⅛ inch in from the edge, leaving the bottom of the piece open. Then stuff the piece, taking care not to overstuff, and sew the bottom edge. Finally, embroider an outline stitch in black around the entire edge of the pillow, working over the original stitching.

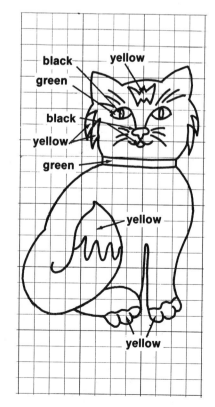

Pattern for pussy cat pillow (1 square = 1")

LONG GREEN CROCODILE— ANOTHER PUPPET

Fierce looking as he is with his bulging eyes and long jagged teeth, children seem to find this crocodile a very funny fellow—especially when they manipulate him to appear as though he's about to bite, and then let him collapse into a helpless little felt heap.

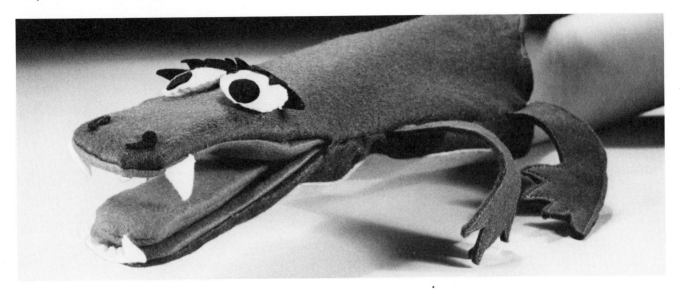

To Make

Enlarge all the pattern pieces for the crocodile to full size (instructions for enlarging are given in Chapter 8). From green felt, cut two main head and body pieces for the crocodile, four front legs, and four back legs; from yellow, one piece for the underbelly; from red, two tongue pieces and two pieces for the inside of the mouth; from white, two upper teeth, one set of lower teeth, and four circles for the eyeballs; and from black, two sets of eyelashes, two nostrils, and two circles for the eyes.

Make each of the front and back legs by placing two corresponding leg pieces together and topstitching around all sides ⅛ inch in from the edges. To assemble the underside of the crocodile, first mark the placement lines for the legs with chalk along the side edges of one of the main head and body pieces, and cut off the tail portion of the piece as indicated by the broken-line markings on the pattern. Set the tail aside but do not discard it. Center the yellow underbelly piece on the main underside piece and topstitch ⅛ inch in from the edge (this will be the right side of the piece). Now pin one of the red inner mouth pieces and the four completed legs to the right side of the crocodile underside piece as shown in the placement and stitching diagram, positioning

Materials

- ¼ yd. 72"-wide green felt
- 6" x 14" piece of yellow felt
- 10" x 12" piece of red felt
- scraps of black and white felt
- small amount of polyester fiberfill stuffing
- green, red, and white sewing thread
- white glue

the legs between the chalk marks with the feet pointed toward the center of the body. Stitch each leg to the main piece ⅛ inch in from the edge. Then stitch the mouth to the main piece ⅛ inch in from the curved outer edge (do not sew along the straight inner edge of the mouth).

To assemble the top side of the crocodile, pin the other inner mouth piece and the reserved tail piece to one side of the remaining main head and body piece for the crocodile, and stitch ⅛ inch in from the outer edges (do not seam the straight inner edges of the mouth and tail pieces). Now pin the assembled underside and top crocodile pieces together, with the underbelly, legs, and red mouth pieces facing to the inside. Seam along each side, stitching ⅛ inch in from the edge between the points marked on the pattern. Turn the main pieces right side out, and then turn the mouth pieces and the tail piece to the inside. Stuff the tail lightly and seam the open end.

Seam together the two red tongue pieces ⅛ inch in from the curved outer edge, leaving the straight back edge open. Turn the piece right side out, stuff lightly, and close the open end with a whipstitch. Now place the tongue in the crocodile's mouth and whipstitch it to the inner mouth piece of the lower jaw along the back edge. Close the mouth and invisibly seam together the sides of the upper and lower jaws for about ¾ inch beyond the end of the previously stitched side seams. Then fold back the upper jaw to this point and invisibly seam together the back edges of the inner mouth pieces.

To finish the puppet, whipstitch two white circles together for each eyeball, stuffing lightly as you sew, and glue the black circles for the eyes in place on the eyeballs. Then glue the nostrils, and sew the eyeballs, eyelashes, and teeth in place on the crocodile as shown in the photograph.

green crocodile underside piece (right side)

stitch→

back leg

yellow underbelly piece

back leg

←stitch

stitch→ front leg front leg ←stitch

red inner mouth piece

stitch→

Placement and stitching diagram for underside of crocodile

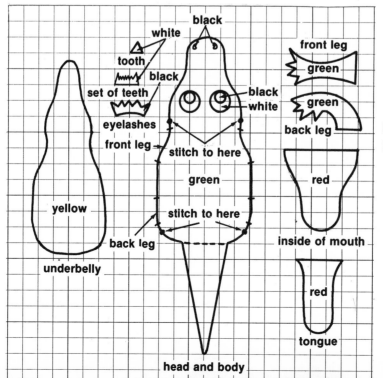

black

white

tooth

black

set of teeth

eyelashes

front leg

stitch to here

green

stitch to here

back leg

underbelly

yellow

head and body

front leg

green

green

back leg

black
white

inside of mouth

red

red

tongue

Pattern pieces for crocodile puppet (1 square = 1")

78

YOUR NAME SHAPES A SPECIAL PILLOW

Our Andy's pillow spells out his name in large orange letters edged with green yarn. Four paper letters were overlapped to make the pattern for this pillow, which measures about 11 inches by 27 inches when finished. You can make a pillow spelling out whatever name you choose by sketching the particular letters you need. The materials listed here are given in the amounts necessary to make a four-letter pillow, and if you wish to spell out a longer or a shorter name, you must remember to adjust the amounts accordingly.

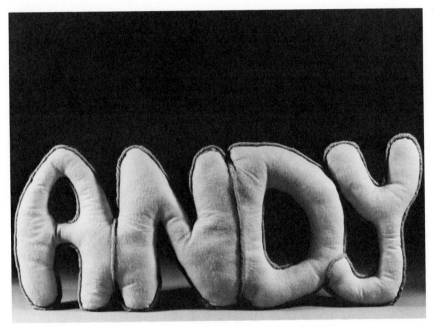

Materials
- 1/3 yd. 72"-wide orange felt
- 2 oz. green bulky yarn
- 1 lb. polyester fiberfill stuffing
- orange and green sewing thread

To Make

Make a paper pattern measuring approximately 8 inches by 11¾ inches for each letter you will need. As you sketch each letter, round off the corners and curve the outer edges so you can overlap them at least ½ inch. Cut out the letter patterns and lap the first letter over the second, the second over the third, and so forth. Adjust the overlap so the letters look balanced, and then tape or pin them together.

Cut two felt rectangles, each approximately 1 inch wider than the height of your letters and 1 inch longer than the length of the spelled-out name. Then, using the pattern, trace off the name onto one piece of the felt, including all the internal openings and edges of the letters. Place the marked piece on top of the other felt rectangle, pin to hold, and then cut out the name, including the internal openings in or between the letters.

Sew the two pieces together around the outer edges and the internal openings with a whipstitch, making the stitches about ⅛ inch deep and stuffing the piece as you sew. Then outline the outer and internal edges of the piece, as well as the demarcations between the letters, with the yarn, and whipstitch the yarn in place with self-color thread.

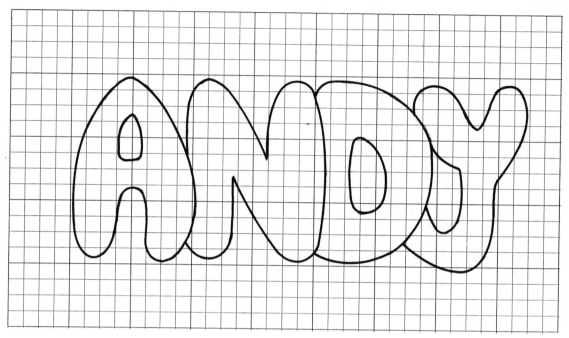

Pillow pattern (1 square = 1")

HIS AND HER CLOTHES HANGERS

One of the hangers shown here is for a little boy and the other is for a little girl. The more of them you make for the boys and girls you know, the more you will be encouraging them to be neat—as well as giving them the pleasure of owning something very special of their own.

Materials for Each Hanger
- 8″ square of flesh-tone felt
- 8″ square of yellow felt
- scraps of blue, white, and pink felt
- small amount of red medium-weight knitting yarn
- 15″ x 19″ piece of heavyweight cardboard or foam-core board
- white glue
- Size G crochet hook
- utility knife

Additional Materials for Her Hanger
- ½ yd. 72″-wide red felt
- 1 oz. red medium-weight knitting yarn
- black marking pen
- red crayon

Additional Materials for His Hanger
- ½ yd. 72″-wide blue felt
- 8″ square of red felt
- 1 oz. blue medium-weight knitting yarn

To Make
Enlarge the pattern for the hanger you wish to make to full size (instructions for enlarging are given in Chapter 8).

Cut the cardboard or foam-core board in the shape of the hanger with a utility knife, following the outline of the pattern. Then from red or blue felt, depending on which hanger you are making, cut a piece to cover one entire side (the back) of the hanger; and using the color key as a guide, mark the outline of the various pattern pieces for the front of the hanger on felt of the appropriate color, and cut out the pieces.

Glue the large red or blue felt piece to one side of the cardboard hanger. Then position all the remaining pieces on the other side of the hanger as shown on the pattern, layering them as necessary, and glue them in place. To finish the hanger, crochet two chains with red or blue yarn, one of them long enough to fit around the outer edges of the front side of the hanger (excluding the head), and the other one long enough to fit around the edges of the hooked top portion of the hanger. Glue the chains in place. Finally, on her hanger, mark eyelashes with the blacking marking pen, and apply a little rouge to the cheeks with the red crayon.

Pattern for his clothes hanger (1 square = 1″)

Pattern for her clothes hanger (1 square = 1″)

FUNNY LITTLE MEN RIDE ON A CHOO-CHOO

This colorful little toy freight has an engine, a coal car, and a caboose, with a motorman and two little trainmen waving to say hello.

To Make

Enlarge the patterns for the engine, coal car, and caboose to full size (instructions for enlarging are given in Chapter 8). Trace the smokestack, cowcatcher, engineer, trainman, and letter patterns. From blue felt, cut two pieces for the sides of the engine, following the outline of the engine pattern, one 5-inch by 25½ inch strip for the front, top, and back of the engine, and one 5-inch by 10½-inch rectangle for the bottom of the engine; from yellow, cut two pieces for the sides of the coal car, following the outline of the coal car pattern, one 4-inch by 18-inch strip for the front, top, and back of the car, and one 4-inch by 8-inch rectangle for the bottom of the car; and, from red, cut two pieces for the sides of the caboose, following the outline of the caboose, one 3½-inch by 17½-inch strip for the front, top, and back of the caboose, and one 3½-inch by 6½-inch rectangle for the bottom of the caboose.

Now, using the color keys on the patterns as guides, on felt scraps of the appropriate color mark the outline of the various pattern pieces for four trainmen, two engineers, two sets of letters spelling "CHOO CHOO," two of each of the windows and wheels on the cars, two smokestack pieces, and one cowcatcher. Also mark one 4-inch-in-diameter circle on yellow felt for the engine headlight, and one 1½-inch-

Materials

- ¼ yd. 72"-wide blue felt
- ¼ yd. 72"-wide yellow felt
- ¼ yd. 72"-wide red felt
- 10" x 20" piece of black felt
- scraps of flesh-tone and white felt
- 10" x 15" piece of medium-weight cardboard
- 2 oz. black medium-weight knitting yarn
- 1 oz. white medium-weight knitting yarn
- 1 2/3 yds. black ball fringe
- 1 small red pompon or piece of ball fringe
- 2 lbs. polyester fiberfill stuffing
- blue, yellow, red, and black sewing thread
- white glue
- large-eyed embroidery needle
- Size G crochet hook
- utility knife

in-diameter circle on black felt for the top of the smokestack, then cut out all the pieces; and from cardboard, cut one 5-inch by 10-inch rectangle for the bottom of the engine, one 4-inch by 8-inch rectangle for the bottom of the coal car, and one 4-inch by 6½-inch rectangle for the bottom of the caboose.

To assemble each car of the train, fit the long felt strip between the two pieces for the sides to form the top, front, and back of the car, and then seam ⅛ inch in from the edges. Now fit the rectangle for the bottom to the bottom of the car and seam around three sides ⅛ inch in from the edges. Turn the car right side out and stuff it firmly. Then insert the appropriate cardboard rectangle through the opening to form a firm bottom, and seam the open side. Finish the engine by seaming the smokestack with a whipstitch, stuffing the piece, and then whipstitching it to the top of the engine as shown in the photograph.

To trim each car of the train, crochet chains with black yarn long enough to fit around all the edges except for the bottom edges of the sides of the car, and glue the chains in place. Then crochet two black chains the length of each car and glue them to the sides of the car along the wheel lines, as shown on the patterns. Embroider the bars of the cowcatcher, and the inner rim and spokes of each wheel with white yarn, using a straight stitch. Glue the cowcatcher and the yellow headlight circle to the front of the engine, and glue the red pompon in the center of the circle. Now arrange one set of window, wheel, trainman, engineer, and letter pieces on each side of the appropriate cars, and glue them in place as shown on the patterns. Then cut the black pompons from the fringe and glue them on top of the coal car to look like a mound of coal. Finally, with four strands of black yarn, crochet two 5-inch chains, and sew them in place as connecting links joining the engine to the coal car and the coal car to the caboose.

Pattern pieces for choo-choo train (1 square = 1")

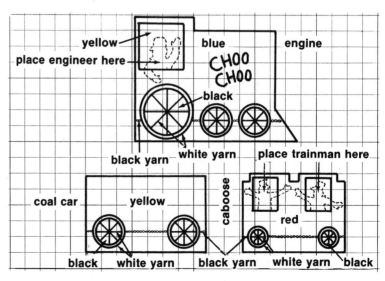

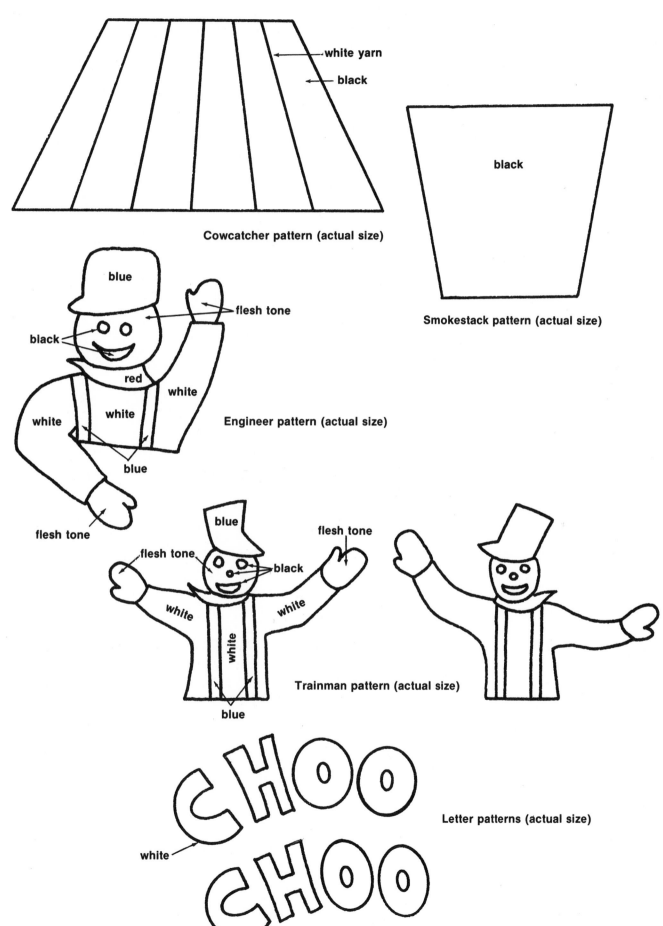

Cowcatcher pattern (actual size)

white yarn

black

black

Smokestack pattern (actual size)

blue

flesh tone

black

red

white

white

white

blue

flesh tone

Engineer pattern (actual size)

blue

flesh tone

flesh tone

black

white

white

white

blue

Trainman pattern (actual size)

CHOO
CHOO

white

Letter patterns (actual size)

85

BIG CHEST FOR STORING LITTLE TOYS

There's room for many playthings in this large, attractively decorated chest, which is made by covering an ordinary cardboard storage box with royal blue felt and decorating the lid with a handful of gaily colored balloons and felt letters that spell the words "MY TOYS" or the name of a child.

Materials

- 1¼ yds. 72"-wide royal blue felt
- 10" x 20" piece of yellow felt
- 6" x 12" piece of orange felt
- 6" square of white felt
- 6" square of red felt
- 2 oz. white medium-weight knitting yarn
- 1 12" wide x 28" long x 16" deep cardboard storage box
- double-faced adhesive tape
- white glue
- Size G crochet hook

To Make

Prepare paper patterns for 3-inch-high letters to spell "MY TOYS" or, if you prefer, a child's name, drawing the letter patterns freehand or enlarging letters from the block letter alphabet in Chapter 6; then from blue felt, cut one 20-inch by 56-inch piece and one 20-inch by 28-inch piece to cover the sides of the box, and one 21-inch by 37-inch piece to cover the lid. To decorate the lid, cut the 3-inch letters to spell "MY TOYS" or the child's name from yellow, following the outlines of the letter patterns, and six 5¼-inch circles for balloons, two each from yellow and orange, and one each from red and white.

Fit the 56-inch-long piece of blue around three sides of the box (one long side and the two short ones), allowing the excess to extend equally beyond the top and bottom edges and the sides, and cutting holes in the felt to accommodate the handles on the chest, if any. Fold the two side edges of the felt around the corners and secure them to the fourth side of the box with strips of double-faced tape. Then turn the extended top edge to the inside of the box and the bottom edge under the box and secure them with strips of the tape.

Cover the lid of the box with the 21-inch by 37-inch piece of blue felt, taking care to fold the felt under neatly at the corners. Secure the turnunder to the inside of the lid with the double-faced tape. Then position the letters and the balloons on the lid as shown in the photograph and glue them in place. With the white yarn, crochet six chains, each one long enough to extend from the bottom of a balloon to the lower left corner of the lid. Position the chains as shown in the photograph and glue them in place. Then crochet one 15-inch chain, tie it into a bow, and glue the bow over the gathered balloon chains as shown. Finally, crochet one chain long enough to fit around the top edges of the lid and another one to fit around the bottom edges, and glue these chains in place.

5.
HOME ACCESSORIES

A few chapters back, by turning the pages of this book we ventured together into a chic little specialty shop that featured all kinds of felt wearables, displaying accessories on the main floor and fashion clothing one flight up. Now, in this chapter, we'll visit the little shop just next door, which also has many unusual things in it, all of them made of felt. It is called the Home Boutique, and in it you'll find a display of charming home accessories, all of them designed for you to make and all created especially for this book. I think you'll find that many of these accessories will look well in your own home, and that others are wonderful for gift giving.

Like all the projects in this book, clear and simple start-to-finish instructions are given for making each of the articles featured in this chapter. You have the option, of course, of making them in the particular colors and decorating them with the trimmings shown here or, if you prefer, of choosing other colors and trimmings of your own. The smaller, though no less important, accessories of the group are shown first, and as you turn the pages you will find larger projects to work on. I hope you will want to make some—and possibly even all—of them.

CALLA LILIES

Looking nearly real, these lovely lilies require little more than scraps of felt and a few lengths of wire. Materials and instructions are given here for making six of them.

Materials
- 12" x 24" piece of white felt
- 12" x 15" piece of green felt
- scraps of orange felt
- 2 yds. 12-gauge florist's wire
- 1½ yds. 16-gauge florist's wire
- 2½ yds. 18-gauge florist's wire
- small amount of polyester fiberfill stuffing
- white, green, and orange sewing thread
- white glue

To Make
Trace the petal and leaf patterns for the calla lily. Cut six petals from white felt, each time folding the felt double, placing the pattern on the fold line as indicated by the pattern marking, and cutting through two thicknesses. From green felt, cut twelve leaf pieces, following the outline of the pattern, and six ½-inch by 10¼-inch strips for the stems; and from orange cut six ½-inch by 2¼-inch strips for the stamens. Then cut six 12-inch lengths of 18-gauge wire for the petals, six 8-inch lengths of 16-gauge wire for the leaves, and six 12-inch lengths of 12-gauge wire for the stems.

To make each flower, shape and glue a length of the petal wire just inside the edge of half the felt petal piece, then fold the other half of the petal on the fold line and glue it over the wired portion of the petal. Fold the orange felt strip for the stamen in half lengthwise and whipstitch the edges together along the long side and one of the short sides, stuffing the piece lightly with fiberfill as you sew.

Then insert a stem wire into the stamen and fold a green felt stem piece around the stem wire, lapping the top of the stem over the base of the stamen. Whipstitch the side and bottom edges of the stem together, and tack the top edge to the base of the stamen. Wrap the base of the completed petal around the base of the stamen, and secure the petal by winding white thread tightly around its base. Cover one side of a leaf generously with glue, set a leaf wire down the center of the glued piece, and glue a second leaf over the wired one. Finally, position the leaf on the stem as desired, secure it in place with a small piece of the 18-gauge wire, and glue a scrap of felt over the wire.

place on fold

Calla lily petal pattern (actual size)

Calla lily leaf pattern (actual size)

QUILTED FELT FRAMES A MIRROR

Very traditional in feeling, this quilted felt mirror frame is trimmed at the corners and around the edges with self-color cord, and is finished with a bow of the same cord to give it that extra little touch. Measuring 22 inches square, with a 12-inch-square mirror set in the center, it will look good hanging on a wall or standing, easel-backed, on a vanity or small occasional table.

Materials

- ¾ yd. 72"-wide cocoa brown felt
- ¾ yd. 45"-wide polyester quilt batting
- 6 yds. dark brown cord
- 12" square mirror, unframed
- 20" square of ¼" plywood
- double-faced adhesive tape
- contact cement
- brown sewing thread
- white dressmaker's carbon paper
- tracing wheel
- table easel or 2 screw eyes and picture wire

To Make

Enlarge the pattern for the mirror frame to full size, including the cutting and hem fold line for the mirror opening and all stitching lines for the quilting (instructions for enlarging are given in Chapter 8), then cut two 25-inch squares of felt and one 25-inch square of quilt batting. With white dressmaker's carbon paper, transfer all pattern markings to one of the felt pieces, extending the quilting lines to the edges of the piece (instructions for transferring pattern markings are also given in Chapter 8).

Keeping the marked felt piece on top, place the batting between the two pieces of felt, pin the three layers together, and stitch the quilting pattern (preferably by machine), following the order of lines indicated on the pattern; then stitch around the marking for the shaped outer edge of the piece, and trim this edge to within ⅛ inch of the stitching. Now cut out the 10-inch center square along the lines marked on the pattern, and clip the corners diagonally, cutting just up to the hem fold line markings. Turn the edges around the mirror opening under along the fold lines, and hem them to the wrong side of the piece.

To trim the mirror frame, arrange four strips of the brown cord diagonally at the corners as shown in the photograph, and stitch them in place; then sew cord around the inner and outer edges of the piece, and sew a bow of cord in place as shown.

Finish the frame by glueing the mirror to the center of the plywood, and then taping the quilted frame to the plywood, making sure that the corded inner edges of the frame overlap the edges of the mirror. Finally, attach the screw eyes and picture wire to the back of the plywood, or stand the mirror on an easel.

Pattern and quilting diagram for mirror frame (1 square = 1″)

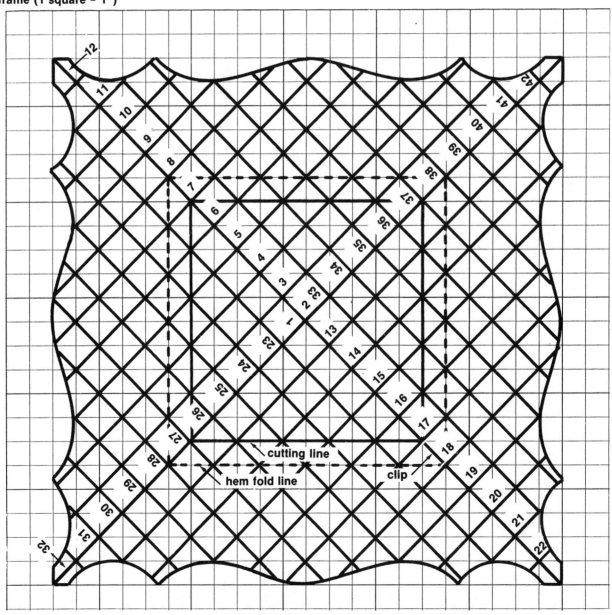

92

SET OF BOOK COVERS

All the covers of this three-piece set are trimmed with the same three-color scroll appliqué motif, but the design has been placed differently on each individual cover so that while each one is attractive and can be used by itself, a completely different effect is achieved when three covered books are placed next to each other on a shelf. Each part of the set will fit a 5¾-inch by 8¾-inch book with a 1¼-inch spine, and directions are also given for adjusting the measurements to fit books of other sizes. The set shown here was made in aqua with camel, burnt orange, and cocoa brown scrolls—but you can, of course, use colors of your own choice.

Materials
- 1/3 yd. 72"-wide aqua felt
- ¼ yd. 72"-wide burnt orange felt
- ¼ yd. 72"-wide cocoa brown felt
- ¼ yd. 72"-wide camel felt
- 1 yd. fusible bonding material
- aqua sewing thread

To Make

Enlarge the patterns for the scroll appliqué motifs to full size (instructions for enlarging are given in Chapter 8), then cut three pieces for the covers from aqua felt, each piece measuring 9 inches by 17 inches (or the actual height of your book plus ¼ inch by the actual width of the front and back covers and spine plus 4 inches for overflaps); and, using the color key as a guide, cut three of each of the scrolls from felt of the appropriate color. Cut a piece of bonding material in the same shape as each of the felt scrolls.

Fit one of the aqua felt pieces around each book, allowing for a 2-inch overlap at each end, and whipstitch each overlap to the outside of the cover along the top and bottom edges. Then place each of the felt scroll pieces on top of a corresponding piece of bonding material, arrange the scrolls on each of the covers as shown in the placement diagram, and affix them to the covers with an iron as directed on the package of bonding material.

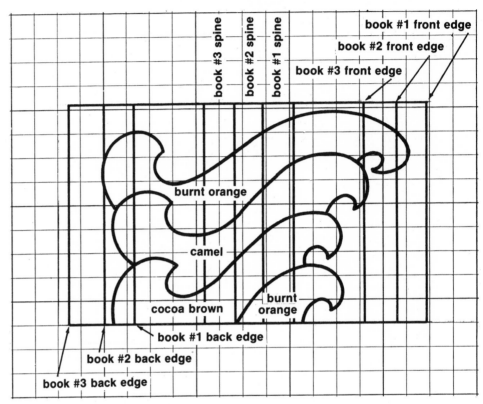

Scroll patterns and placement diagram (1 square = 1″)

ATTRACTIVE DESK SET

The letter file, pencil holder, paper clip holder, and desk blotter of this set have been designed with a two-color checkerboard pattern, which is woven of felt strips to make it just a little different. It is an elegant looking set, although very easy to make and requiring very few materials other than a small amount of felt, a blotter, some cardboard, and a few additional odds and ends that you're likely to find, oddly enough, in your kitchen.

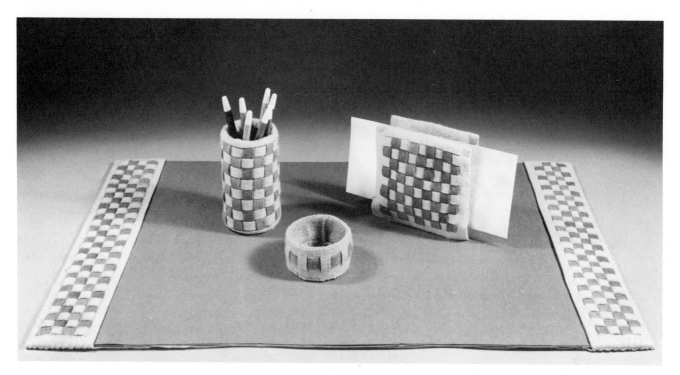

To Make

Cut from aqua felt: for the letter file, two 5-inch by 5½-inch pieces and two 4¼-inch by 5½-inch pieces; for the pencil holder, one 6-inch by 9-inch piece, and one circle 2¾ inches in diameter; for the paper clip holder, two 1½-inch by 9½-inch strips and two circles 2¾ inches in diameter; for the blotter, two 3-inch by 16-inch strips and one 16-inch by 27-inch piece.

Then cut the medium blue felt into a number of ½-inch by 16-inch strips to be used, as needed, for weaving all the items in the set.

To assemble the letter file, first prepare the 5-inch by 5½-inch pieces of aqua felt for weaving by cutting slits in each piece. Cut the slits parallel to the lengthwise edge, leaving a ½-inch border on all sides and spacing the slits ½ inch apart. Now weave strips of the medium blue felt in and out of the slits of each aqua piece, leaving the borders free.

Materials

- ½ yd. 72″-wide aqua felt
- ¼ yd. 72″-wide medium blue felt
- 16″ x 27″ desk blotter
- 16″ by 27″ piece of medium-weight cardboard
- 1½″ x 9½″ strip of medium-weight cardboard
- 1 empty 12-oz. frozen juice can
- 1 paper napkin holder with 5″-square sides
- 1 2¾″-in-diameter jar lid
- aqua sewing thread
- double-faced adhesive tape
- white glue

Cut the weaving strips as necessary and tack the ends of each strip in place on the underside of the work with aqua sewing thread. To finish the letter file, sew each woven piece, right side out, to one of the 4¼-inch by 5½-inch plain felt pieces, sewing around three sides with a whipstitch and leaving one of the 5½-inch-long sides open; then slip the finished pieces over the sides of the napkin holder.

To assemble the pencil holder, cut lengthwise slits in the 6-inch by 9-inch piece of aqua felt, leaving a 1-inch border along the long edges and a ½-inch border along the short edges, and spacing the slits ½ inch apart. Weave strips of medium blue felt in and out of the slits and tack the ends in place in the same manner as described for the letter file. Seam the short ends of the woven piece together with a whipstitch, using aqua sewing thread. Finish the bottom of the pencil holder by seaming the aqua felt circle to the woven piece around one edge. Finally, slip the juice can, closed end down, into the piece, turn the extended top edge of the felt to the inside of the can, and secure it with double-faced tape.

To assemble the paper clip holder, cut short widthwise slits in one of the 1½-inch by 9½-inch strips of aqua felt, leaving a ½-inch border on all sides and spacing the slits ½-inch apart. Weave a single strip of medium blue felt in and out of the slits and tack the ends in place as described for the letter file. Join the two short ends of the woven piece with a whipstitch, then whip together the ends of the plain 1½-inch by 9½-inch aqua felt strip. Place the plain felt ring inside the woven one and whip the pieces together around one edge. Now tape the 1½-inch by 9½-inch strip of cardboard around the jar lid to build up the sides, and slip the completed felt ring over the cardboard. Finally, glue one of the aqua felt circles to the inside of the lid, then place the other circle under the lid and whipstitch it to the bottom edge of the woven felt ring.

To assemble the blotter, cut short widthwise slits in each of the 3-inch by 16-inch pieces of aqua felt, leaving a ½-inch border free on all sides and spacing the slits ½ inch apart. Now weave strips of medium blue felt in and out of the slits and tack the ends in place in the same manner as described for the letter file. Place the woven pieces right side up on the 16-inch by 27-inch felt rectangle, one at each side edge. Align and then whipstitch the three outer edges of each woven piece to the edges of the large rectangle. Finally, slip the large cardboard rectangle and then the blotter into the felt holder.

OLD-FASHIONED BELL PULL PUT TO A NEW USE

Cut from a small strip of felt and backed with cardboard, this cross-stitch-embroidered bell pull makes a perfect backdrop for a few of your favorite photographs or miniature paintings. It is finished with a decorative single crochet edging worked through blanket stitches, and has a tassel to trim its pointed bottom end. The one shown in the photograph was made in camel and cocoa brown, but you can make yours to coordinate with your own color scheme.

Materials

- ¼ yd. 72"-wide camel felt
- 2 oz. cocoa brown medium-weight knitting yarn
- 5" x 30" piece of medium-weight cardboard
- white glue
- large-eyed embroidery needle
- Size G crochet hook

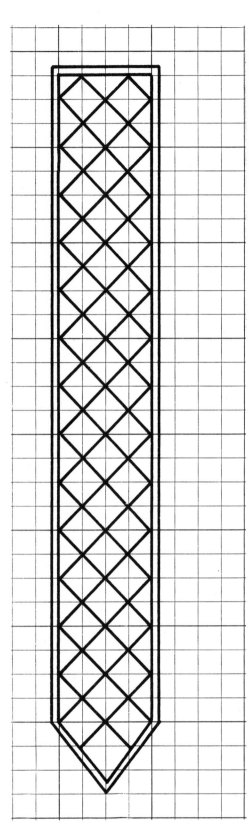

Pattern for bell pull (1 square = 1″)

To Make

Enlarge the pattern for the bell pull to full size, including all the markings for the cross-stitch design (instructions for enlarging are given in Chapter 8).

Cut one bell pull from felt and another from cardboard, following the outline of the pattern, then lightly transfer the pattern markings to the felt piece (instructions for transferring pattern markings are also given in Chapter 8).

Embroider the edges of the felt strip with blanket stitches, making the stitches ¼ inch deep and spacing them ¼ inch apart. Work a row of single crochet through the blanket stitches, working three single crochet into one blanket stitch to turn each corner (the blanket stitch and single crochet edgings are illustrated in the section on edgings and joinings in Chapter 3). Now, using the lines marked on the felt as a guide, embroider large cross stitches on the front of the piece as shown in the cross stitch diagram; then work a couching stitch over the intersections of the cross stitches as shown in the couching diagram.

Make a tassel for the finished piece by wrapping a length of yarn about twenty times around a 6-inch square of cardboard. Tie the strands together at one edge of the cardboard, leaving ends long enough to sew the tassel to the bell pull, and cut through the strands at the other edge of the cardboard. To finish, wind a piece of yarn several times around the tassel 1 inch down from the top, then knot and trim the ends, and the tassel of the point at the bottom. Then, finally, glue the finished piece to the cardboard backing, and trim it with your photographs or paintings (mounted in four 2¼-inch by 3¼-inch gold frames and one 4-inch by 5-inch frame as shown here, or as you desire) by attaching a small loop to the back of each frame and tacking the loops to the bell pull.

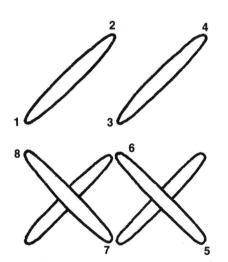

Cross stitch diagram. Draw needle up at odd-numbered points, insert needle at even-numbered points

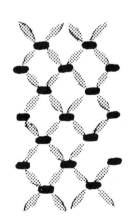

Couching diagram

98

BUTTERFLY MOBILE

Bright, colorful felt butterflies hang on a mobile to delight the heart of any young child who watches them dangling from their perches and flying at the slightest breeze. Seven large butterflies and four small ones, in vivid aqua and burnt orange, were used to make the mobile pictured here, but for your own mobile you can make as many butterflies in whatever colors and sizes you like.

Materials

- ¼ yd. 72"-wide aqua felt
- ¼ yd. 72"-wide burnt orange felt
- 2 oz. black medium-weight knitting yarn
- small amount of polyester fiberfill stuffing
- 10 black pipe cleaners
- 1 small gold ring
- 2 6"-in-diameter circular wooden hoops
- transparent nylon thread
- aqua, orange, and black sewing thread
- white glue

To Make

Trace the large and small butterfly patterns; then cut fourteen large butterflies, six from aqua felt and eight from burnt orange felt, and eight small butterflies, six from aqua and two from burnt orange.

To make each butterfly, place two pieces of the same color and size together and whipstitch around the edges with self-color thread, leaving a small opening for stuffing. Stuff the piece firmly and whip the open edges together; then decorate the wings of all the joined pieces with black yarn as shown on the patterns, cutting a strand for each one long enough to fit around both wings and glueing it in place. Outline the entire edge of each butterfly with black yarn and whip the yarn in place with black sewing thread. Make a body for each one by winding black yarn around the center portion, building up a big body on the large butterflies and winding only once or twice around the small ones. To make antennae for each large one, cut two 3-inch pieces of pipe cleaner, place one on each side of the body so the ends extend well beyond the front edges of the wings, and whip them in place with black thread. Cut two 1½-inch pieces of pipe cleaner for each small one and attach them in the same way. Then curl the antennae of the large butterflies and bend the antennae of the small ones as shown.

To assemble the mobile, cut four 12-inch strands of transparent nylon thread. Knot one end of each strand to one of the wooden hoops, spacing the strands evenly around the circumference of the hoop, then take the other ends of the strands and knot them together through the gold ring to make a hanging loop. To suspend the second hoop, cut four additional 12-inch strands of nylon thread and, spacing them evenly, knot one end of each strand through the first hoop and knot the other end around the second hoop. Finally, to hang the butterflies, cut fourteen strands of nylon thread in varying lengths, stitch one end of each strand to the top of a butterfly and tie the other end around one of the hoops as shown in the photograph.

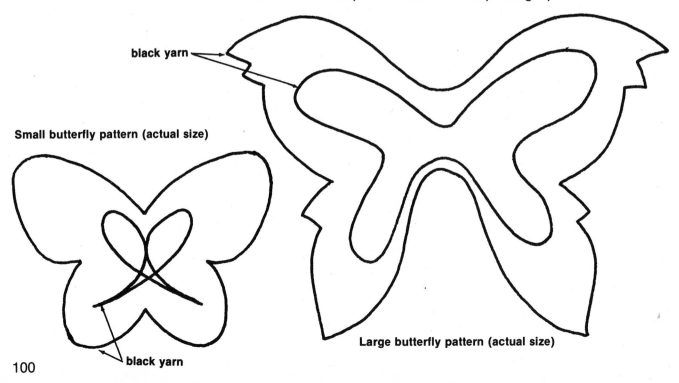

black yarn

Small butterfly pattern (actual size)

black yarn

Large butterfly pattern (actual size)

DECORATIVE TRAY HOLDER

With pockets to hold two 10-inch trays, this attractive tray holder will look good hanging on your kitchen or dining room wall. It is made from a few narrow strips of felt, appliquéd with sunflowers and finished with a few bands of rickrack in a contrasting color.

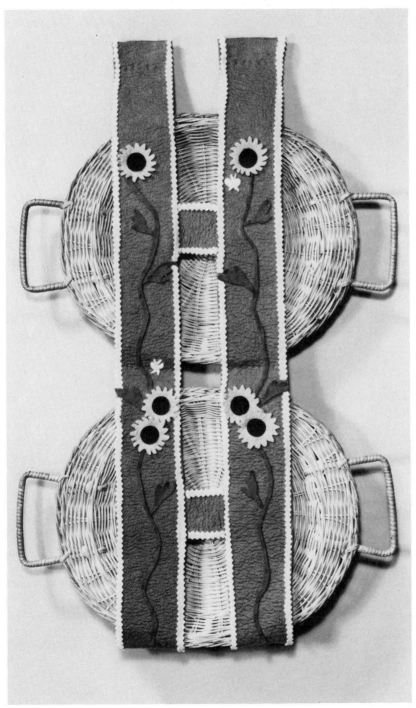

Materials

- ¼ yd. 72"-wide dark brown felt
- scraps of burnt orange, white, yellow, green, and black felt
- 3 yds. narrow beige rickrack
- 1 12" hanging rod
- dark brown sewing thread
- white glue

To Make

Trace the sunflower pattern shown in the flower section of Chapter 6, and then reduce it to half the original size (instructions for reducing a pattern are given in Chapter 8). From brown felt, cut two 2½-inch by 48-inch strips for the vertical straps of the tray holder, and four 3-inch by 2-inch strips for the cross pieces, then cut six sunflowers from burnt orange, and six round sunflower centers from black.

Sew the short ends of each long felt strip together securely, and arrange the doubled strips so the stitched seams fall at the center back. Make a top casing for the hanging rod by stitching across each doubled strip 1¼ inches down from the folded top end, and a support for the base of the top tray by stitching across each doubled strip 11 inches up from the folded bottom end. Now arrange one small felt cross piece between the two finished straps 6¾ inches down from the top ends and another cross piece 4 inches up from the bottom ends, and stitch them securely in place under the edges of the front layers of the straps. Arrange and stitch the remaining two cross pieces to the back layers of the straps at the same distance from the top and bottom ends.

Glue the black centers to the orange sunflowers, then glue the completed flowers to the straps of the tray holder as shown in the placement diagram. From green felt, cut vines and leaves freehand to fit; and from white and yellow, cut tiny butterflies freehand. Glue these in place, then finish the tray holder by stitching rickrack along all the edges of the front side of the piece as shown in the photograph.

Placement diagram for sunflower appliqué trim

MULTIPOCKETED WALL HANGING

This easy-to-make wall hanging for a child's room would delight any youngster even if it didn't have secret pockets worked into its cheerful appliquéd motifs. There's a clown holding tight to a balloon with a pocket just right for crayons, a cherry-topped ice-cream cone with a triangular pocket for storing scissors, a plastic-lined sailboat for pennies, and a schoolhouse and three-pocketed car for hiding all sorts of childhood valuables.

Materials

- ½ yd. 72"-wide camel felt
- scraps of aqua, red, burnt orange, cocoa brown, white, and black felt
- scrap of clear medium-weight plastic
- ¼ yd. ¾"-wide white eyelet trim

To Make

Enlarge the appliqué patterns for the wall hanging to full size (instructions for enlarging are given in Chapter 8). Then from camel felt, cut one 18-inch by 26-inch piece for the backing of the hanging, then, using the color key as a guide, mark the outline of the various pattern pieces for the appliqué motifs on felt scraps of the appropriate color, and cut out the pieces. From clear plastic, cut a semicircle slightly larger than the pattern piece for the bottom of the boat.

- 5 yds. narrow black cord
- ¼ yd. narrow white cord
- 16" x 24" piece of ¼" plywood
- orange, aqua, brown, and white sewing thread
- masking tape
- white glue
- 2 screw eyes and picture wire

Glue the door and window pieces to the white felt pocket piece for the schoolhouse appliqué. Now, leaving a 1-inch border around all sides of the camel felt backing, glue all the felt appliqué pieces to the backing as shown on the pattern, except for the car wheels and the pocket pieces, which are marked "sew" on the pattern. Arrange the felt pocket appliqués for the ice-cream cone, car, schoolhouse, and balloon, and the clear plastic pocket for the sailboat as shown on the pattern and whipstitch or machine stitch them securely to the backing, leaving the top edge of each pocket open. Topstitch two vertical seams on the large pocket of the car to divide it into three equal-sized sections, and then glue the wheels in place on the car.

To finish the hanging, glue small pieces of eyelet as ruffles around the clown's neck and feet as shown in the photograph, and glue bits of white cord to the shoes as shoelaces. Arrange pieces of black cord on the backing of the hanging to form the smoke coming from the schoolhouse chimney, the waves around the boat, and the balloon string, and glue the cords in place. Glue black cord to accent the edges of the schoolhouse and car pockets, the sail, the balloon, the ice-cream cone, and the arms and body of the clown, as shown in the photograph. Finally, mount the hanging on the plywood rectangle, turning under the 1-inch border on all sides and securing it to the back of the plywood with masking tape. Attach two screw eyes and picture wire.

Appliqué patterns and placement diagram for wall hanging (1 square = 1")

color key:
A = aqua F = white
B = black G = clear plastic
C = orange H = white cord
D = brown I = black cord
E = red

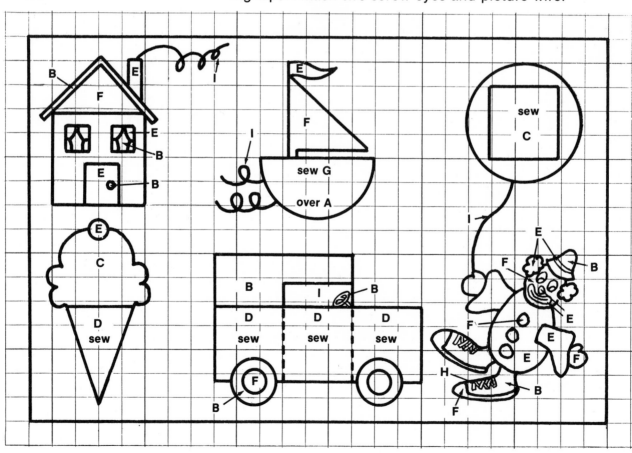

LAMP

It may surprise you to learn that this interesting lamp base is really a juice can—empty, of course. It was wired and fitted with the necessary hardware (available at hardware stores), covered with a piece of felt, trimmed with three-dimensional felt rounds in three different colors, and then topped with an attractive store-bought shade. The lamp shown in the photograph was made from a 46-ounce can, but you can make your own lamp as large or small as you like by choosing a can or other cylinder-shaped base of a different size.

Materials
- 9" x 21" piece of camel felt
- scraps of dark brown, aqua, and burnt orange felt
- 1 empty 46-oz. juice can, wired and fitted with 8" harp, bulb socket, and finial
- 1 suitable lamp shade
- white glue

To Make

From camel felt, cut an 8-inch by 15-inch rectangle and a circle measuring 4¼ inches in diameter (or, if the cylinder you plan to cover is a different size, measure its height and add 1 inch, measure its circumference and add ¼ inch, and cut a rectangle of these dimensions; then cut a circle large enough to cover the top of the cylinder). For the trim, cut sixty ¼-inch by 6-inch strips of felt, ten from burnt orange, thirty from aqua, and twenty from dark brown.

To cover the lamp base, wrap the camel felt piece around the can, leaving an equal amount extending beyond the top and bottom edges, and glue it in place. Fold the excess felt under the bottom end of the can and glue it to the inside of the can. Clip into the excess felt around the top of the can at ½-inch intervals, then fold the clipped segments over the top of the can and glue them down. To accommodate the hardware, cut a center hole and a slit in the circle of camel felt, then glue the circle to the top of the can.

Make the three-dimensional trim for the lamp by spreading glue on one side of the narrow felt strips and rolling the strips into rounds. Position and glue the different-colored rounds to the lamp base as shown in the placement diagram, repeating the pattern five times around the top and bottom of the base, or as many times as necessary for your own base. Finally, top the lamp with the shade.

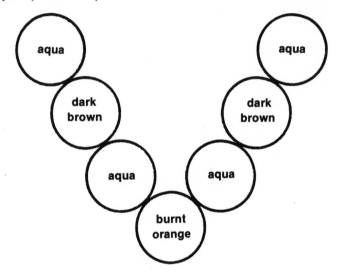

Placement diagram for lamp trim

ROUND TABLECLOTH

The beauty of this lovely tablecloth belies the ease with which it can be made. Little more is required than cutting the pieces, appliquéing the tulip and leaf motifs around the edges of the cloth, and then contouring the edge with a scissors. While the cloth shown in the photograph is a 46-inch round, once you've read the simple instructions, you can make yours any size you wish.

To Make

Trace the patterns for the tulip and leaf appliqués. From dark brown felt, cut a circle measuring 46 inches in diameter (or the desired size). And, following the outlines of the patterns, cut sixteen tulips each from burnt orange felt and bonding material, and sixteen leaves each from aqua felt and bonding material.

Materials
- 1 1/3 yds. 72"-wide dark brown felt
- ¼ yd. 72"-wide aqua felt
- 16" square of burnt orange felt
- 1½ yds. fusible bonding material
- 7 skeins of orange 6-strand embroidery floss
- 6 skeins of royal blue 6-strand embroidery floss
- embroidery needle

Embroider chain stitches on each of the felt tulip and leaf pieces along the lines marked on the patterns, using burnt orange floss for the tulips and royal blue floss for the leaves. Now, divide the large circle for the tablecloth into sixteen equal-sized segments and mark these divisions along the edge of the cloth with pins. Place the tulips and leaves, right sides up, on top of the corresponding pieces of bonding material. Arrange the tulips and leaves around the cloth close to the edge, centering one flower and leaf in each of the sixteen pin-marked segments, and fix them to the cloth with an iron as directed on the package of bonding material. Finally, contour the edge of the cloth with a very sharp scissors, cutting as close as possible to the appliquéd tulip and leaf trim.

Placement diagram for tulip and leaf appliqués

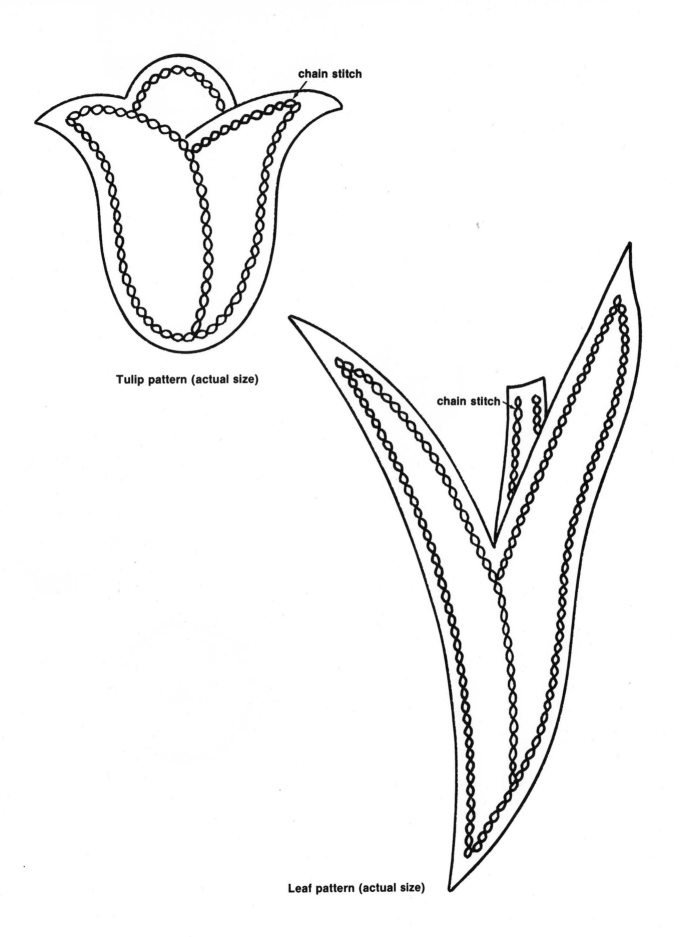

chain stitch

Tulip pattern (actual size)

chain stitch

Leaf pattern (actual size)

COVERED PARSONS TABLE FOR CHIC DECOR

Felt-wrapped legs and a two-color bordered top disguise an inexpensive table and give it a look of upholstered elegance. This one is a 16-inch-square plastic table with removable legs for easy storage, and once you've read the easy directions, you can give the same treatment to any size or kind of square or rectangular table that you'd like to dress up.

Materials

- ¾ yd. 72"-wide camel felt
- ¼ yd. 72"-wide burnt orange felt
- ¼ yd. 72"-wide dark brown felt
- 1 16" Parsons table with 16" removable legs
- camel, burnt orange, and dark brown sewing thread
- double-faced adhesive tape

To Make

From camel felt, cut one 18-inch square for the table top and four 2-inch by 72-inch strips for the leg wrappings. To trim the sides of the table top, cut four 16-inch by ¾-inch strips from burnt orange and eight 16-inch by 1¼-inch strips from dark brown.

110

To make the trim for each side of the table top, stitch together one burnt orange and two dark brown strips as shown in the border trim placement and stitching diagram. Now cut out a 1-inch square from each of the four corners of the camel piece for the table top, and topstitch one of the completed border strips to each side of the square, lapping the long inner edge of each strip 1 inch over the edge of the square and stitching close to the inner edge of the strip as shown in the diagram. Sew the corners together from the right side of the piece with a whipstitch.

Apply strips of the double-faced tape to each side of all the table legs, then, working from the bottom up, wrap one of the 72-inch felt strips around each of the four legs, wrapping diagonally and overlapping the edges. Cut away the excess material at the top of each leg. Finally, slip the cover over the table top, securing the bottom edges with tape, and attach the legs.

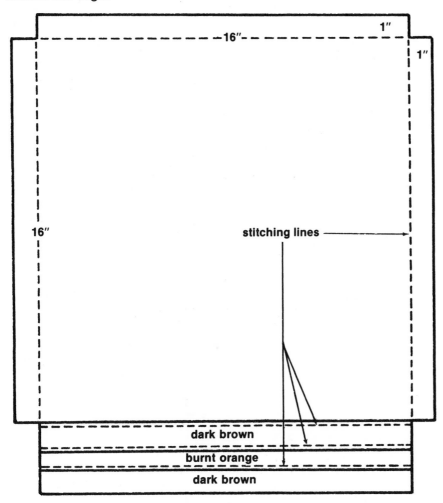

Placement and stitching diagram for table trim

COMFORTABLE-TO-SIT-ON, FRIENDLY-TO-BE-WITH HASSOCK

The 12½-inch-square cube shown here would be a most welcome addition to any youngster's room. A simple plywood box covered with squares of felt in three different colors, the hassock has a friendly puppy appliquéd on one of its sides, and alphabet letters and numbers on the other sides.

Materials

- ½ yd. 72"-wide camel felt
- ½ yd. 72"-wide white felt
- ½ yd. 72"-wide aqua felt
- 1/3 yd. 72"-wide brown felt
- scraps of black and red felt
- 5 yds. dark brown cord or braid
- 1 12½"-square ¼"- plywood cube
- dark brown sewing thread
- white glue

To Make

Trace the puppy pattern shown in the animal section of Chapter 6, and enlarge it to 10½ inches, using a scale of ¼ inch equals ¾ inch. Choose a combination of five letters and numbers from the block letter alphabet and the number chart in the same chapter and enlarge them to 10½ inches, using a scale of ¼ inch equals 3½ inches (instructions for enlarging are given in Chapter 8). Now cut six 13-inch squares of felt, two in camel, two in aqua, and two in white.

Cut the main piece for the body of the puppy appliqué, and each of the letter and number appliqués you have chosen, from dark brown. Cut the puppy's paws, chest fur, muzzle, and eyeballs from white; cut the tail, eyes, eyebrows, top-lock, and ears from black; and cut the mouth and collar from red.

Sew five of the felt squares together, wrong sides out, to form a cube. Stitch by hand or machine ¼ inch in from the edges, alternating camel and white squares on the four sides of the cube, using an aqua square on the top, and leaving the bottom open. Turn the piece right side out and insert the plywood cube into it. Then hand stitch the second aqua felt square in place over the open bottom of the cube, folding each edge of the square under ¼ inch as you stitch.

Glue the pieces of the puppy appliqué in place on one of the camel-color sides of the cube. Then arrange the number and letter cutouts on the remaining sides and glue them in place. Finally, sew the brown cord around all the edges of the cube over the seams joining the felt squares, as shown in the photograph.

6.
TRIMS

"Plain" is a word often used to describe something that is dull, uninteresting, and not very pretty—like a cake without a frosting. And just as a frosting can turn a plain cake into a piéce de résistance, so, too, can a decorative trim transform an ordinary garment or home accessory into a chic and fashionable one.

Felt is a perfect material for making many different trims, and you will probably find that the designs in this chapter will inspire you with all kinds of new "felt art" ideas. The golf and tennis motifs, for example, make excellent decorations for a sportsman's room or clothing; the felt animals are just right for embellishing a pet lover's things; and the very real-looking flowers make pretty additions to a plain skirt or sweater.

Yes, there is fun for everybody here, including myself who has had so much pleasure designing the various motifs appearing on the pages that follow, and who would like to note now just a few suggestions and reminders that might open even more avenues of creative thought to you. You already know that you can edge felt pieces in a number of interesting ways. You should also remember that since the material will neither ravel nor fray, you can use it just as it is, and you can add felt trimmings to anything by simply stitching them to your background material, glueing them in place, or ironing them on with pieces of bonding material cut in the same shape as the felt pieces. Remember, too, that you can make any of the designs as small or as large as you like, and directions for doing this are given in Chapter 8. If you wish to give your trimmings a layered three-dimensional look when working any of the designs in which some portions overlap others, do this by tracing each of the different parts of the design separately, then cutting those that are to be overlapped slightly larger than actually called for in the pattern. And, finally, where fine lines are used in a design, these are best shown with simple embroidery stitches or with pieces of narrow cord or braid stitched or glued in place.

PERSONALIZE WITH YOUR OWN ABC'S

If you want to make something very specially your own, monogram or spell out your name on it, using the block or script letters shown here, or a combination of both. Trimming things with letters is fun, and there are many creative ways to do it. Try decorating a blanket, for instance, by randomly spacing the first letter of your name all over it; personalize a tote bag with a monogram and surround the initials with flowers or a border chosen from the designs in this chapter, or finish a sweater or jacket with initials, or perhaps with a meaningful word, placed just above the ribbed cuff of one sleeve.

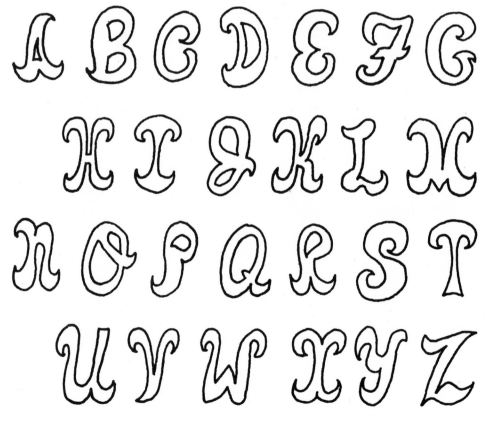

A B C D E F G
H I J K L M
N O P Q R S T
U V W X Y Z

Block letter alphabet

A B C D E F G
H I J K L M
N O P Q R S T
U V W X Y Z

Script letter alphabet

COUNT YOUR BLESSINGS — OR ANYTHING ELSE

Now that you've learned your ABC's, you might also enjoy remembering in felt that 1 + 1 = 2, and 2 × 2 = 4. Such simple mathematical equations, cut from the number patterns shown here, perhaps along with a few simple words like "cat" and "zoo" spelled out in capital letters, would make a charming "learning board" wall hanging for a small child's room; and for more serious business, you might make a wall plaque showing an important date and a message commemorating a birth, anniversary, or other special occasion that you want to remember permanently, or to enliven a kitchen, consider a colorful hanging with the ingredients and quantities of a favorite recipe worked out in felt numbers and letters, perhaps embellished with a few luscious felt fruits cut from the patterns shown later in the chapter.

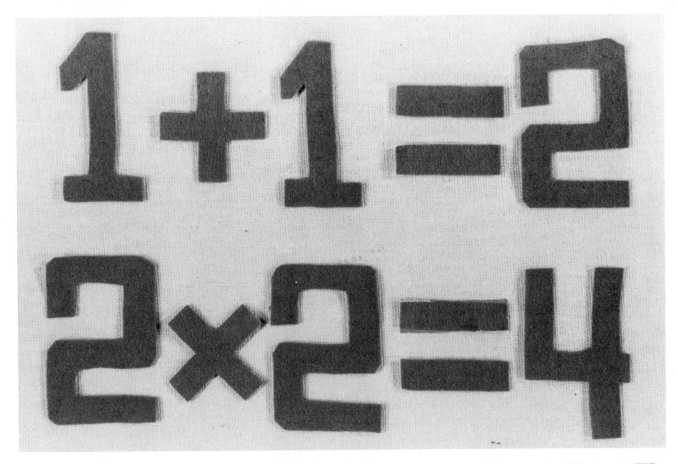

Number patterns

FLOWERS TO BEAUTIFY EVERYTHING

Use these flowers singly, scatter them, or create a mixed bouquet to trim a robe, lamp shade or hamper; or glue them to the plain painted wall of a bathroom or kitchen to make it one of the most attractive and unusual rooms in the house.

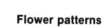

Flower patterns

SMALL CREATURES

While "God made us all, both big and small," still there are some of us who can't stand the sight of tiny crawling creatures. The special whimsical-looking group here, however, is really very cute, and what is more they are guaranteed not to crawl. They make wonderful mobiles, and are fun to use to trim walls, hampers, closet accessories, planters, and many other household items, as well as to decorate jackets, skirts, jeans, sweaters, and other wearables.

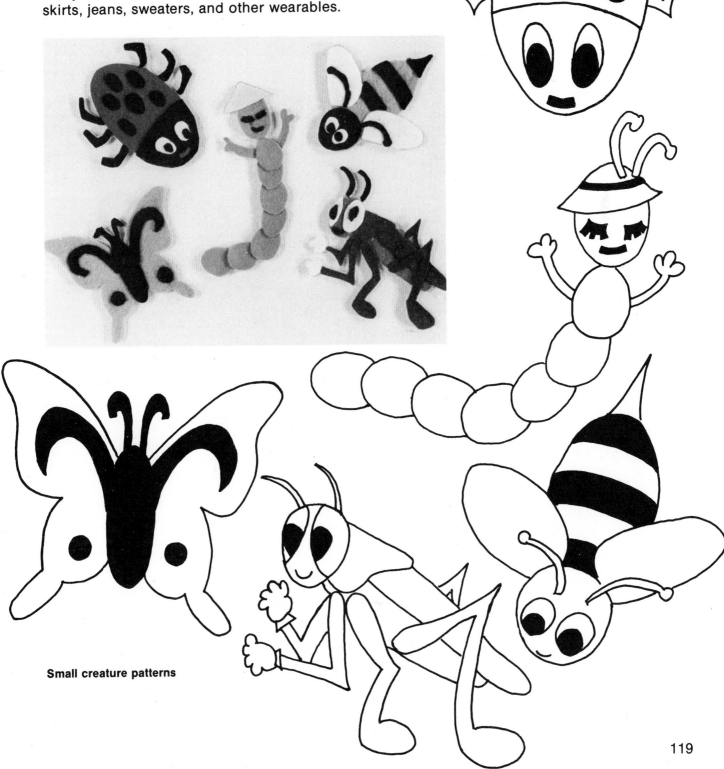

Small creature patterns

Anyone would be happy to have something of his of her very own decorated with these heavenly body cutouts. A large shooting star appliquéd on a jacket or knapsack is certain to please a small boy very much. You could delight a little girl by stitching a smiling sun or a winking crescent moon to her favorite jeans or skirts and make her big sister happy with a sweater decorated with a monogram encircled by stars. These are just a few suggestions for using the astral cutouts, and you are sure to come up with many other design ideas of your own.

Heavenly body patterns

Little Jack Horner and some of his nursery rhyme pals are here, waiting to befriend all small children who have heard their tales and would like to get to know them better. You can help to cement the friendship by creating a mobile out of one or all of them, or by glueing them in an interesting arrangement to a wall or window shade, a pillow or hassock, or a toy chest or laundry bag.

Nursery rhyme patterns

123

ANIMALS FOR LITTLE PEOPLE AND PET LOVERS

A puppy for dog fanciers, a friendly feline for cat lovers, a pony for the horsey set, and a ferocious tiger and performing elephant complete with circus tent are all gathered here to spark your creative imagination. Think of making a large wall hanging with an entire family of cats, perhaps a large mother cat with three or four of her kittens around her; or embellish a lamp shade with a trotting pony; or make a felt "painting" for a wall of your child's room, using ponies, lions, elephants, and a circus tent, all surrounded by a colorful border emblazoned with the legend "TOMMY'S CIRCUS"—substituting your own child's name, of course.

Animal and tent patterns

125

PENNSYLVANIA DUTCH FOLK ART

Contrasting sharply with their simple, even austere, way of life, the rich and highly developed folk art of the Pennsylvania Dutch people is filled with brilliant colors and whimsical designs. No one who has wandered through these Pennsylvania farming communities or has seen examples of their household crafts can ever forget the immaculate barns with their bold star-and-circle "hex" sign decorations, the peacock-painted walls, the chests and furniture trimmed with sprightly hearts and scrolls, and the exquisite flower-garlanded quilts. An example of the Pennsylvania Dutch peacock, heart and flower design, scroll, and the famous hex sign are shown here. They are easy to adapt into patterns for trimming a piece of clothing or something in your home and, whether you use them individually or in combination, they make lovely designs for anything you choose to put them on.

Pennsylvania Dutch patterns

127

FRUITS IN AND OUT OF SEASON

Looking good enough to eat, these luscious felt fruits can be used in many different ways to add decorative touches to your kitchen or dining room. They make attractive appliqués for a set of solid-color place mats, coasters, or kitchen equipment covers, and you can use a different fruit for each piece of the set. They also make very unusual wall decorations. A still life of large oranges, pineapples, and bananas, for example—perhaps with a bee (or any of the other small creature cutouts) hovering above and a border pattern surrounding the entire composition like a frame—could make a lovely hanging for an informal dining room; while a ripe watermelon, "painted" on with glue, would add a cheerful touch of color to a plain kitchen wall.

Fruit patterns

GOOD SPORTSMANSHIP

Trim a cap or covers for your woods and irons with a golf emblem, spruce up a racquet cover with a felt tennis cutout, or use one of the other motifs shown here on the gear for your own—or someone else's—favorite sport. Large initialed skis would make a solid-color jacket look very special, as would a pin-and-ball design on a bowling bag, or a baseball and bat on anything in the room of a strong young outfielder.

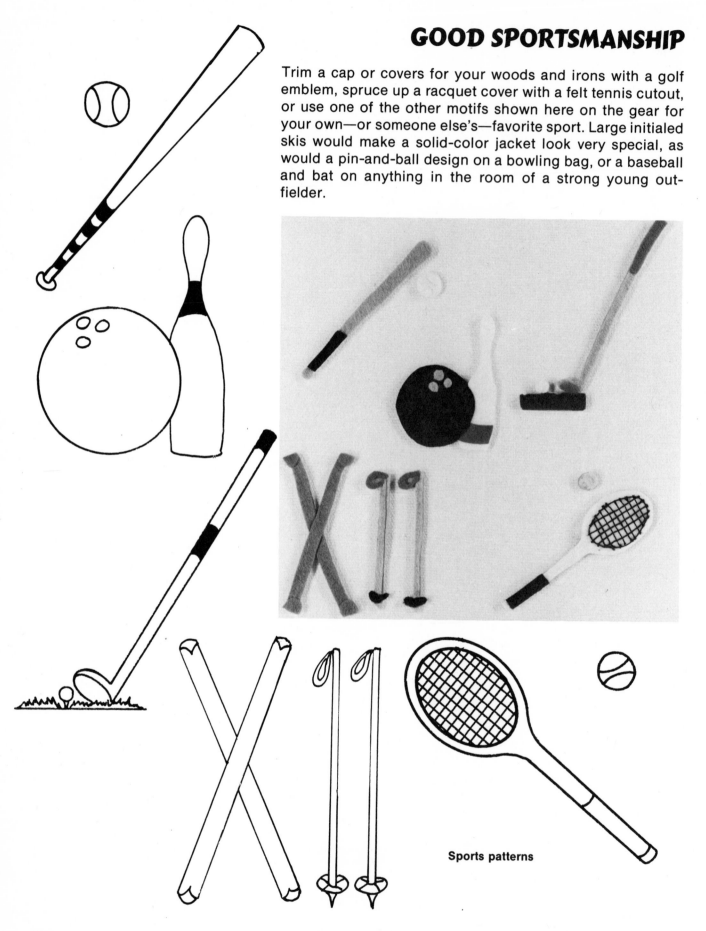

Sports patterns

BORDERS

These versatile border designs are perfect for giving a final finishing touch to a new project you are making or to something old that needs a bit of refurbishing. Place them around the entire hemline of a skirt, tablecloth, or bedspread, or add them to the cuffs and the collar or neckline of a sweater, blouse, or jacket; or perhaps use them to frame a wall hanging, or trim a pillow, or just add small bits and pieces of them to accent something you want to really stand out.

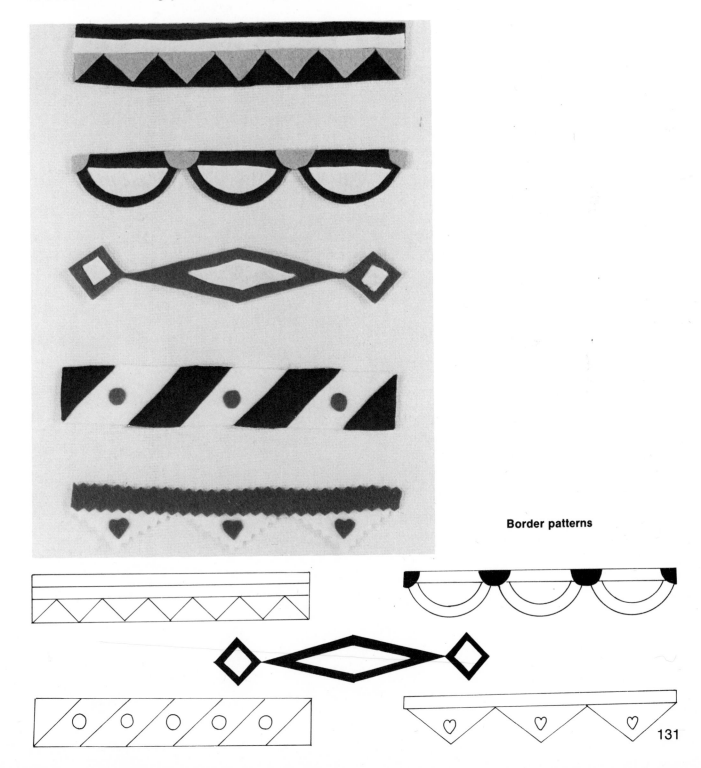

Border patterns

131

Three Trimmed Projects

Now that you've been introduced to the world of trimming with felt, you may be interested in seeing a few examples of how the designs shown in this chapter have actually been used to decorate some very plain and unexciting things—a toaster cover, a small pillow, and a child's windbreaker, turning them into eye-catching designer articles.

BOWLING BALLS AND PINS TRIM A BOY'S JACKET

Any of the sports motifs shown in this chapter can be used to make something very special out of a plain jacket, T-shirt, or pair of jeans. The back of the boy's jacket photographed here was trimmed with two bowling-ball-and-pin appliqués, one of them traced directly from the pattern shown in the sports section of this chapter, and the other one enlarged to three times the original size. The appliqués can be affixed to the jacket with fusible bonding material, or they can be tacked on around the edges with sewing thread so they can be easily removed any time the garment needs to be washed.

ATTRACTIVE TOASTER COVER

An ordinary, perfectly plain toaster cover is transformed into something rather special by decorating it with one of the Pennsylvania Dutch appliqué motifs, and accenting the appliqué with a small strip of border trim. This cover could be part of a lovely set, including blender, electric mixer, and cookie jar covers, all trimmed with the same motif in the arrangement shown here, or perhaps each cover of the set decorated with a different but coordinated design.

FUN PILLOW

A circus tent and ball-balancing elephant made from patterns shown in the animal section of this chapter, framed by a few lengths of one of the border trims, turn this 12-inch-square solid-color pillow into a delightful room accessory. The same trim can be used to decorate a larger pillow, and in this case you would probably want to enlarge the appliqué motifs and use two rows of the border trim all around.

7.
CHRISTMAS ACCESSORIES

Elf's Slipper Stocking

Santa's Mukluk

Candy-Striped Tights

Madam's High-Buttoned Shoes

Traditional Stocking—Personalized,
Of Course!

Poinsettias Bloom on an Around-the-Tree Rug

Glittering Wreath

Frosty the Snowman and Frieda His Friend

Pretty Garland for Your Tree

Santa Claus Mobile

Robinson the Reindeer

A Pretty Angel

Carrot-Nosed Snowman

Fancy Gingerbread Folk

A joy for all of us, Christmas is a time of gladness, giving, and good cheer. The bustle of preparations for the great day usually starts weeks in advance as presents are bought and made and closets are filled to overflowing with mysterious boxes and bundles. Anticipation builds as holiday decorations are retrieved from the attic and the annual assortment of new things is added. And when tantalizing once-a-year aromas begin wafting from the kitchen and the house is decked out with festive decorations, everyone knows the waiting is almost over. Finally, just when it seems hardly possible to contain the excitement—especially of the children—any longer, that very special Night Before arrives, signaling the real start of the fun. The tree makes a regal appearance in its accustomed corner and, accompanied by a chorus of stage directions, is gleefully dressed in its finery. Then, with great expectations, the stockings are hung, everyone goes to bed, and "not a creature is stirring all through the house," until quietly and joyously, Christmas arrives.

As you prepare for this festive season, I hope you'll browse through my very special felt Christmas Boutique. Here you'll find a variety of delightfully different decorations that will add to the cheerfulness of your home at that good time of the year. Some of the things are whimsical and refreshing, others are simply beautiful. There are unusual stockings to be hung up on Christmas Eve and filled with surprises, a lovely rug to spread under the tree, a glittering wreath for your door, angels and gingerbread men for your tree, and many more things—all designed in felt and very easy to make. I hope they will add pleasure to your anticipation of the holiday as you make them, and that they will give enjoyment to all of your family members and friends who celebrate the holiday with you.

Christmas Stockings

Especially designed for the Night-Before-Christmas fun, these eye-catching stockings are easy to make and perfect for stuffing with candy canes, bonbons, and all those "extra" little packages. All of the them are trimmed on one side only (whichever side you prefer) and, except for the 22-inch candy-striped tights, each one is 14 inches long. You can enlarge the patterns, however, to make them in any size you wish, from little ones for very little people to a mammoth family-sized one—perhaps to be put away in some quiet spot long before the holiday, there to be filled little by little with all the family's gifts, and to be touched and added to day by day until Christmas finally arrives. For each stocking shown, you'll find a list of all the materials you'll need to make it, graphed pattern pieces for the particular project, and actual-size drawings to be traced for the trim.

ELF'S SLIPPER STOCKING

Materials

- 15" x 21" piece of red felt
- 11" x 18" piece of white felt
- scrap of green felt
- small amount of black embroidery thread
- 1½ yds. ¼"-wide metallic gold cord or braid
- 2 yds. ⅛"-wide black cord or braid
- 6 small white pompons or pieces of ball fringe
- red and white sewing thread
- white glue

To Make

Enlarge the three pattern pieces for the stocking to full size (instructions for enlarging are given in Chapter 8). Trace the reindeer and star patterns. Then from red felt, cut two main stocking pieces, following the outline of the pattern for this, and then cut one ¾-inch by 3-inch strip for the tab; from white, cut one piece for the center of the cuff and two pieces for the side of the cuff and one more for the reindeer; and from green cut the star.

Using black embroidery thread, embroider the features marked on the reindeer with an outline stitch. Place the two main stocking pieces together, right sides out, and using red thread, machine stitch (or sew by hand with small running stitches) around the sides and foot of the stocking ⅛ inch in from the cut edges of the felt.

Glue the three sections of the cuff, the reindeer, and the star in place on the stocking as shown in the photograph. Then glue gold braid in place to outline the edges and the center section of the cuff, and to form a bow and two reins for the reindeer. Glue the black braid in place to outline the reindeer, and to decorate the outer edge of the stocking starting and ending just below the cuff. Finally, sew on the pompons, stitching one to each of the three points of the cuff and the remaining three together at the point of the toe. Then fold the tab piece in half to form a loop, and stitch the ends inside the top edge of the cuff near the back seam.

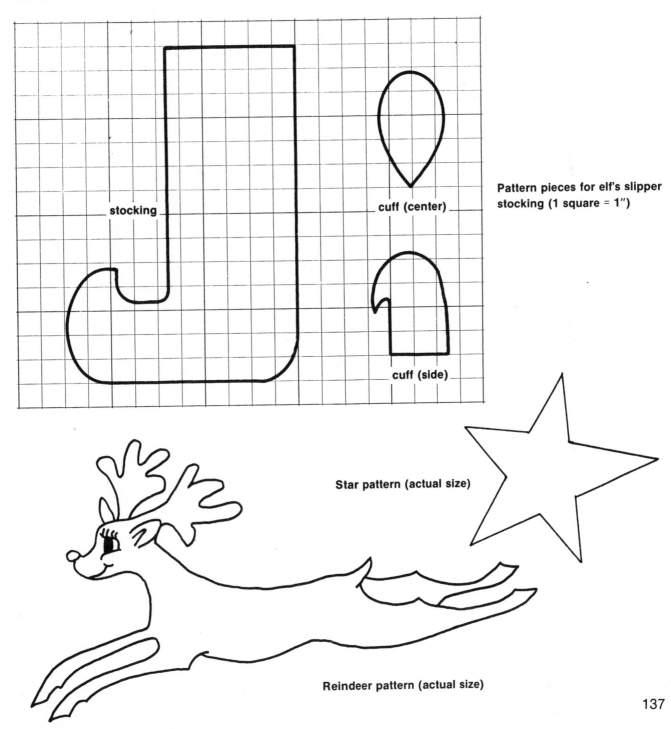

stocking

cuff (center)

cuff (side)

Pattern pieces for elf's slipper stocking (1 square = 1″)

Star pattern (actual size)

Reindeer pattern (actual size)

Materials

- 15" x 21" piece of red felt
- 3" x 11" piece of black felt
- 4" x 6" piece of green felt
- 5½" x 8½" piece of white fake fur or fringed material
- ½ yd. ⅛"-wide black cord or braid
- small amount of metallic silver embroidery thread
- 4 small square white buttons
- 1 small red pompon or piece of ball fringe
- red and white sewing thread
- white glue
- embroidery needle

To Make

Enlarge the two pattern pieces for the stocking to full size (instructions for enlarging are given in Chapter 8). Trace the large and small holly leaf patterns. From red felt, cut two main stocking pieces, following the outline for this, and one ¾-inch by 3-inch strip for the tab. From black, cut one sole and heel piece, following the outline of the pattern, and from green cut two large and one small holly leaves.

Now using the silver embroidery thread, embroider the markings on the leaves with an outline stitch. Sew the four buttons in place on one of the main stocking pieces, starting approximately 6 inches down from the top of the piece and spacing the buttons 1½ inches apart and 1½ inches in from the front edge. Place the two main stocking pieces together and, using red thread, machine stitch (or sew by hand with small running stitches) around the sides and foot ⅛ inch in from the cut edges of the felt. Glue the sole and heel piece in place, and to complete the cuff, position the piece of fake fur or fringed fabric on the stocking just above the top button and glue it in place.

Finally, to make the bootlaces, wind the black braid back and forth between the seam and the buttons as shown in the photograph, and glue it in place; then glue the holly leaves and the pompon in place on the cuff as shown; and fold the tab piece in half to form a loop, then sew the ends inside the top edge of the cuff near the back seam.

Pattern pieces for Santa's mukluk (1 square = 1")

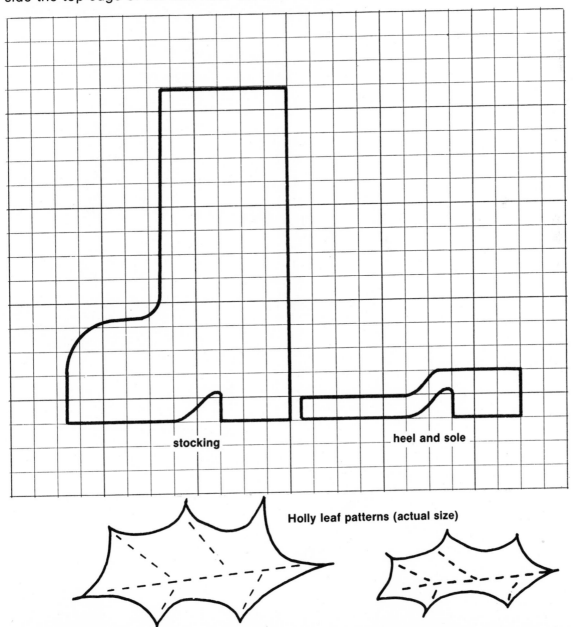

stocking

heel and sole

Holly leaf patterns (actual size)

CANDY-STRIPED TIGHTS

Materials

- 23" x 33" piece of white felt
- scrap of red felt
- 2 yds. ¼"-wide green velvet ribbon
- 7 yds. ¼"-wide red velvet ribbon
- 1 yd. 1"-wide red satin ribbon
- red and white sewing thread
- white glue

To Make

Enlarge the pattern piece for the tights to full size (instructions for enlarging are given in Chapter 8). Then from white felt, cut two stocking pieces, following the outline of the pattern, being sure, when cutting each piece, to fold the felt double; then place the pattern on the fold as indicated by the pattern marking and cut through two thicknesses; and, finally, from red cut two tabs, each measuring ¾ inch by 3 inches.

Place the two stocking pieces together and, using white thread, machine stitch (or sew by hand with small running stitches) around the legs ⅛ inch in from the cut edges of the felt. Cut the green and red velvet ribbons into the lengths needed to arrange them in the position and color pattern shown in the photograph. (Note that the single ribbons are red, and the groups of three consist of a green ribbon in the center with a red ribbon on each side of it.) Pin the ribbons in place and glue them down as pinned, gluing the remaining length of red around the entire outer edge of the stocking. Make a bow with the wide red satin ribbon and sew it to the tights as shown in the photograph, and finally fold the two tab pieces in half to form loops, and sew these in place inside the top edge of the tights, one near each side seam.

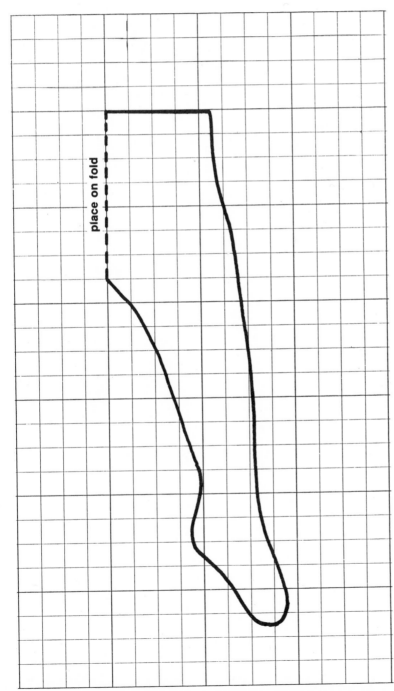

place on fold

Pattern for candy-striped tights (1 square = 1″)

MADAM'S HIGH BUTTONED SHOES

Materials

- 15" x 21" piece of red felt
- 4" x 6" piece of black felt
- scrap of green felt
- 2/3 yd. 1"-wide white gathered eyelet trim
- 1 yd. narrow white cord or braid
- small amount of white embroidery thread
- 8 small round white buttons
- 1 small red pompon or piece of ball fringe
- red sewing thread
- white glue

To Make

Enlarge the three pattern pieces for the stocking to full size (instructions for enlarging are given in Chapter 8) and trace the holly leaf pattern. From red felt, cut two stocking pieces, following the outline of the main stocking pattern, then cut a ¾-inch by 3-inch strip for the tab; from black, cut one heel and one sole, following the outlines of the patterns, and from green, two holly leaves, following the outline of the leaf pattern. Finally cut the eyelet trim into four 5-inch pieces, and cut the white cord into eight 4½-inch pieces.

Now using white embroidery thread, embroider the markings on the leaves with an outline stitch and sew the eight buttons in place on one of the main stocking pieces, starting 4 inches down from the top of the piece, and spacing the buttons 1 inch apart and 1 inch in from the front edge. Seam the two main stocking pieces together on the right side, using red thread and stitching by machine (preferably) or by hand with small, closely spaced running stitches, sewing ⅛ inch in from the cut edges of the felt and leaving the front of the stocking open in the area of the buttons.

To finish, glue the four pieces of eyelet across the top of the stocking to form the cuff, placing one strip below the other as shown in the photograph, and glue the heel and sole pieces in place. Loop one of the 4½-inch lengths of white cord around each button as shown and glue it in place, tucking the cut ends of each loop under the open front edge of the stocking, Then stitch the open portion of the seam by hand. Glue the holly leaves and the pompon in place on the cuff as shown and, finally, fold the tab in half to form a loop, and sew the ends in place inside the top edge of the cuff, near the back seam.

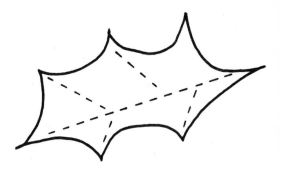

Holly leaf pattern (actual size)

Pattern pieces for high-buttoned shoes (1 square = 1″)

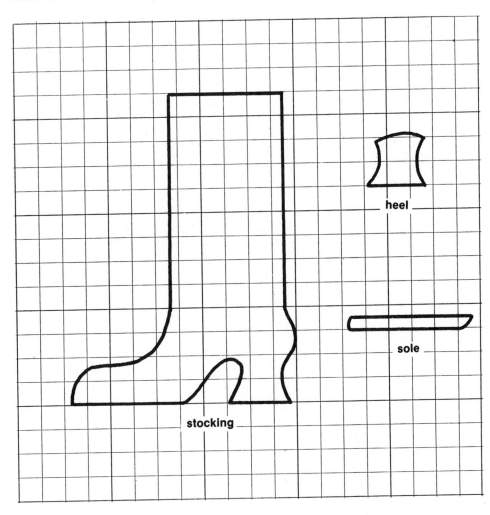

heel

sole

stocking

TRADITIONAL STOCKING— PERSONALIZED, OF COURSE!

Materials

- 15" x 21" piece of red felt
- 8" x 10" piece of white felt
- 5" square of green felt
- scraps of black and pink felt
- 12" strip of green medium-width rickrack
- 1 yd. ⅛"-wide gold metallic cord
- 1½ yds. black braid
- green embroidery thread
- 1 small white pompon or piece of ball fringe
- small amount of polyester fiberfill stuffing
- red, white, and green sewing thread
- white glue
- embroidery needle

To Make

Enlarge the pattern piece for the stocking to full size (instructions for enlarging are given in Chapter 8), then trace the Santa pattern. From red felt, cut two stocking pieces, following the outline of the pattern, and cut one ¾-inch by 3-inch piece for the tab; from white, a 4½-inch by 5½-inch piece for the cuff; and from green, a circle measuring 4½ inches in diameter for the Christmas ball trim. Now, using the color key as a guide, mark the outline of Santa's face, features, cap, whiskers, and beard on felt scraps of the appropriate color, and cut out these pieces.

Complete the Christmas ball trim by glueing the pieces for Santa's face to the green felt circle. Now draw the desired name freehand on the cuff with pencil, and embroider over the markings with a chain stitch, using green embroidery thread. To finish the cuff, glue on strips of rickrack ¼ inch in from the long top and bottom edges as shown in the photograph, then center a length of gold cord on each strip of rickrack and glue it down. Arrange the Christmas ball and the cuff on one of the stocking pieces as shown, and stitch them in place around the edges with self-color thread, stuffing each piece lightly as you sew.

To finish, seam the two stocking pieces together on the right side, using red thread and stitch by machine (preferably) or by hand with small, closely spaced running stitches, sewing ⅛ inch in from the cut edges of the felt, then outline the Christmas ball with gold cord, and glue the cord in place; cut a 4-inch piece of the cord, double it, and glue it as a hanging loop at the top of the ball, and glue the black cord around the entire outer edge of the stocking and across the bottom edge of the cuff. Finally, fold the tab in half to form a loop and stitch it in place inside the top edge of the cuff, near the back seam.

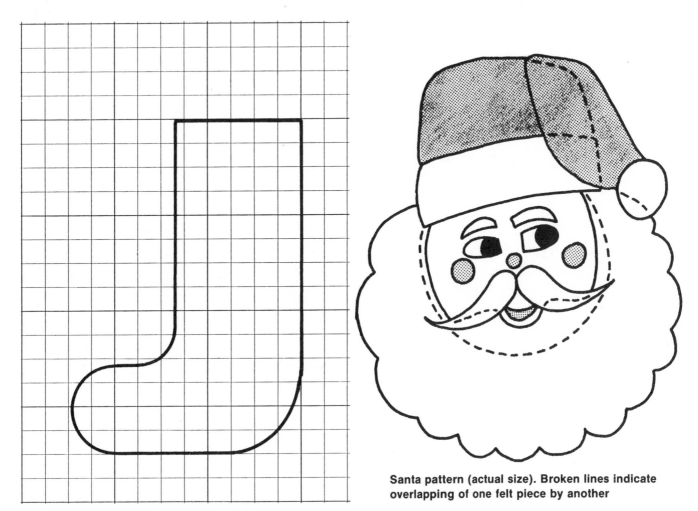

Santa pattern (actual size). Broken lines indicate overlapping of one felt piece by another

Pattern for traditional stocking (1 square = 1")

POINSETTIAS BLOOM ON AN AROUND-THE-TREE RUG

Five big, bold, bright red poinsettias, strategically set on a frosty white background, will make this charming around-the-tree rug a stunning addition to your Christmas decorations. Finished with a very attractive red scalloped border, the rug measures 43 inches in diameter, and has a 5½-inch opening in the center and a slit in the back.

Materials
- 1¼ yds. 72"-wide white felt
- 1 yd. 72"-wide red felt
- ¼ yd. 72"-wide green felt
- 2 oz. white medium-weight knitting yarn
- red sewing thread
- white glue

To Make

Enlarge the pattern for the border to full size (instructions for enlarging are given in Chapter 8). Make two tracings of the quarter patterns for the large and small poinsettias, and make half patterns for each poinsettia by reversing one of the tracings and taping the two quarter patterns together along the dotted line. Trace the leaf and center-nub patterns. From white felt, cut a circle measuring 43 inches in diameter; then cut a small one measuring 5½ inches in diameter from the center of the large one. From red, cut four scalloped border pieces, and one ½-inch-wide circular band to fit around the inner edge of the rug (to do this, cut a 6-inch-in-diameter circle, then cut away a 5-inch-in-diameter circle from the center); and from the remaining red felt, cut five large poinsettias and five small ones, each time folding the felt double, placing the pattern on the fold line as indicated by the pattern marking, and cutting through two thicknesses. Finally, from green cut twenty-four leaves and five center-nub pieces.

Fit the border pieces around the rug, aligning the edges of the openwork scallops with the edge of the rug, and glue them in place. Then contour the edge of the rug with a very sharp scissors, cutting as close as possible to the scalloped edge of the border; fit the circular red band around the center opening of the rug and glue it in place; and starting anywhere along the circumference, slit the rug from the outer edge to the center (this will be the center back opening).

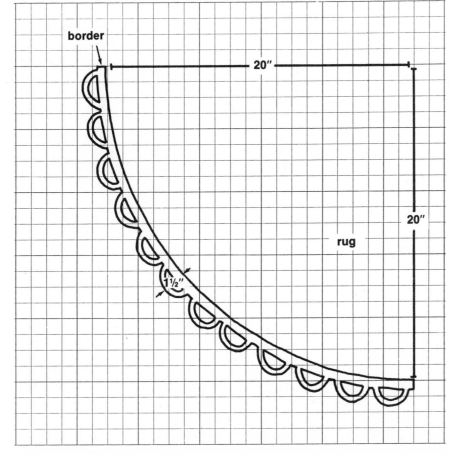

Pattern and placement diagram for scalloped border (1 square = 1″)

147

To assemble the poinsettia decorations, with white yarn embroider seven French knots in the middle of each green center-nub piece, then glue one finished nub in the center of each of the five small poinsettias. Glue one of the small poinsettias on top of each of the large ones, glueing at the center only. Finally, arrange the five finished poinsettias evenly around the rug, placing them about 4 inches in from the border, and glue them down, again applying the glue only at the centers; and arrange and glue the leaves under the edges of the poinsettia petals, using eight leaves around the flower at the center front and four leaves around each of the other four flowers.

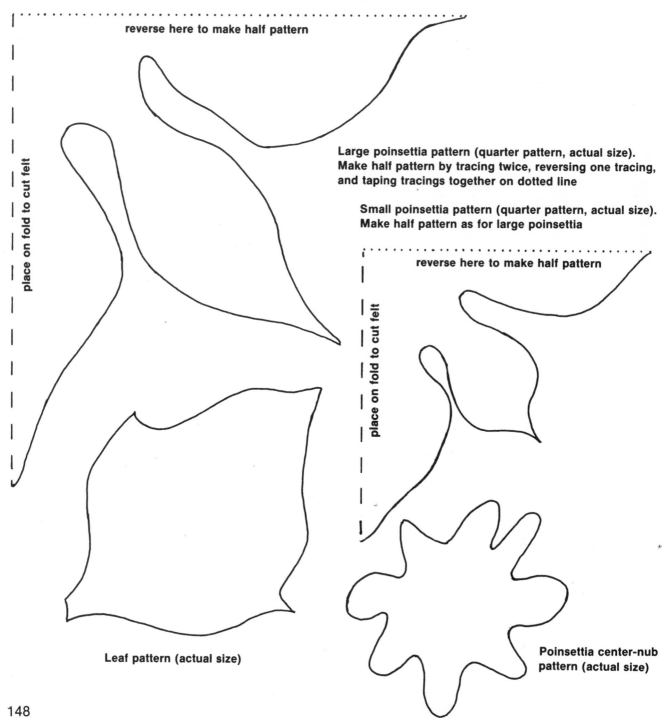

reverse here to make half pattern

place on fold to cut felt

Large poinsettia pattern (quarter pattern, actual size). Make half pattern by tracing twice, reversing one tracing, and taping tracings together on dotted line

Small poinsettia pattern (quarter pattern, actual size). Make half pattern as for large poinsettia

reverse here to make half pattern

place on fold to cut felt

Leaf pattern (actual size)

Poinsettia center-nub pattern (actual size)

GLITTERING WREATH

Simply beautiful, this glistening, glittering holly wreath is practically a work of art, yet it is easy to make and will be one of the most unusual and attractive door decorations your friends and neighbors have ever seen.

Materials
- 1 yd. 72"-wide white felt
- small amount of bulky red yarn
- 3 yds. 3"-wide silver garland
- 2 yds. 3"-wide red satin ribbon
- 2 oz. silver glitter
- 1 lb. polyester fiberfill stuffing
- white sewing thread
- white glue

To Make

Trace the patterns for the large and small leaf clusters and enlarge them to full size (instructions for enlarging are given in Chapter 8). From white felt, cut two circles, each measuring 20 inches in diameter, and then cut a small circle measuring 7 inches in diameter from the center of each large circle.

Place the two large circles together, right sides out, and sew the outer edges together with a whipstitch, then whipstitch the inner edges, stuffing the piece firmly as you sew. Mark seven large and seven small leaf clusters on the remaining piece of white felt, leaving a space of about ½ inch between each cluster and making sure to transfer all the inner markings as well as the outer ones (instructions for transferring pattern markings are also given in Chapter 8).

Go over all the markings with the open point of the glue bottle, sprinkling glitter onto the glue as you go. Allow to dry thoroughly, then gently shake off the excess glitter and cut out the leaf clusters, cutting each piece ⅛ inch outside the outer glitter markings. Glue the center of each small leaf cluster to the center of each large one. From the red yarn, make seven large, loose knots, and glue one knot at the center of each finished leaf cluster, tucking the yarn ends under the knots.

Finally, sew the silver garland in place around the inner and outer edges of the stuffed wreath form; and arrange the seven leaf clusters on the wreath, leaving a 3½-inch space free and overlapping the clusters as necessary; glue the clusters in place, applying the glue only to the centers and leaving the outer points of the leaves free; and sew a large ribbon bow in place to cover the free space on the wreath.

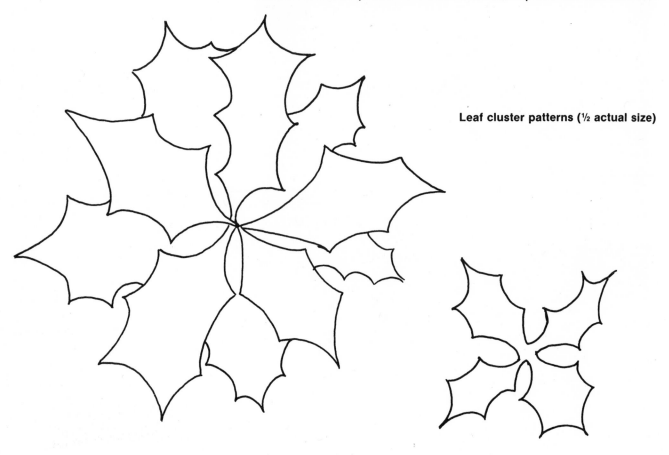

Leaf cluster patterns (½ actual size)

FROSTY THE SNOWMAN AND FRIEDA HIS FRIEND

This happy little snow couple cannot help but add to the festiveness of your holiday. They are made separately and can stand alone or, since they will not melt, they can be forever joyously attached to each other. As shown here, they stand 23 inches tall and are trimmed on one side only, to be made welcome in any corner or against any wall. Should you prefer to stand them somewhere in the middle of a room, however, you can easily trim them on both sides.

Materials for Frosty

- 2/3 yd. 72"-wide white felt
- ¼ yd. 72"-wide red felt
- 12" x 30" piece of black felt
- scrap of green felt
- ½ yd. 1"-wide red satin ribbon
- ½ oz. silver glitter
- 12" x 24" piece of cardboard

To Make Frosty

Enlarge to full size the pattern pieces for Frosty's head and body, arm, and base, and those for the crown and top of his hat (instructions for enlarging are given in Chapter 8), and trace the pattern pieces for Frosty's facial features and the leaf trim for his hat. From white felt, cut two head and

- 1 lb. polyester fiberfill stuffing
- white sewing thread
- masking tape
- white glue

body pieces, four arms, and one base, following the outlines of the appropriate patterns, and four 3-inch by 5-inch strips to trim the scarf; from red, cut four mittens and one mouth, following the patterns for these, and one 5-inch by 36-inch piece for the scarf; from black, one nose, two eyes, two hat brims, and one piece for the top of the hat, following the outlines of the patterns, and one 4-inch by 12-inch strip for the crown of the hat, and four 1-inch by 5-inch strips to trim the scarf; and from the scrap of green cut two leaves; then from cardboard, cut one base, one hat brim, and one piece for the top of the hat, following the patterns, and one 4½-inch by 12-inch strip for the crown of the hat.

Sew the two head and body pieces together, right side out, with a whipstitch, leaving the bottom edge open, then stuff the piece firmly. Trim the edge of the cardboard base ½ inch all around, then center it on the felt piece for the base and glue it in place. Sew the base to the stuffed head and body piece with a whipstitch, tucking in the extended felt edges of the base as you sew. Sew two of the felt arm pieces together for each arm, leaving the top edge open, and stuff firmly, then stitch together the open edges of each arm, forming a flap by sewing first along the inner stitching line marked on the pattern and then along the outer edge. Sew the arms in place, thumbs up, at the sides of the body. To finish the figure, glue all the facial features in place as shown in the photograph.

To make each of the mittens, sew together two of the red felt mitten pieces (leave the tops open) and turn down a 1½-inch cuff, then spread glue over the cuff and sprinkle glitter over the glued surface. Allow to dry thoroughly, then gently shake off the excess glitter. And to complete the scarf, glue one of the 1-inch by 5-inch strips of black felt down the center of each of the 3-inch by 5-inch strips of white felt, then arrange two of these two-color pieces at each end of the red felt scarf piece as shown, and glue them in place.

To make the hat, join the two short ends of the cardboard strip for the crown with masking tape, forming a cylinder, then glue the black felt strip for the crown around the cylinder, leaving ½ inch of the cardboard exposed at the bottom edge. Clip the exposed cardboard at ½-inch intervals and fold the clipped sections outward to form a lip for attaching the brim. Glue one of the black felt brim pieces to the cardboard brim. Slide the brim, felt side up, over the crown, tape the clipped cardboard lip of the crown to the underside of the brim, then glue the other black felt brim piece to the underside of the brim. To finish the hat, trim the black felt piece for the top of the hat ½ inch all around, cen-

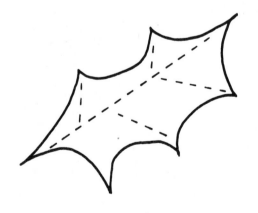

Holly leaf pattern (actual size)

ter it on the corresponding cardboard piece, and glue it down. Clip the exposed edge of the cardboard at ½-inch intervals, and fold down the clipped sections. Fit the top of the hat, felt side up, into the crown and secure it on the inside with masking tape. Vein the green leaves with glue and sprinkle them with glitter, and finally, glue the red satin ribbon around the base of the hat, and trim it with the leaves and the pompon, and dress Frosty with his mittens, scarf, and hat.

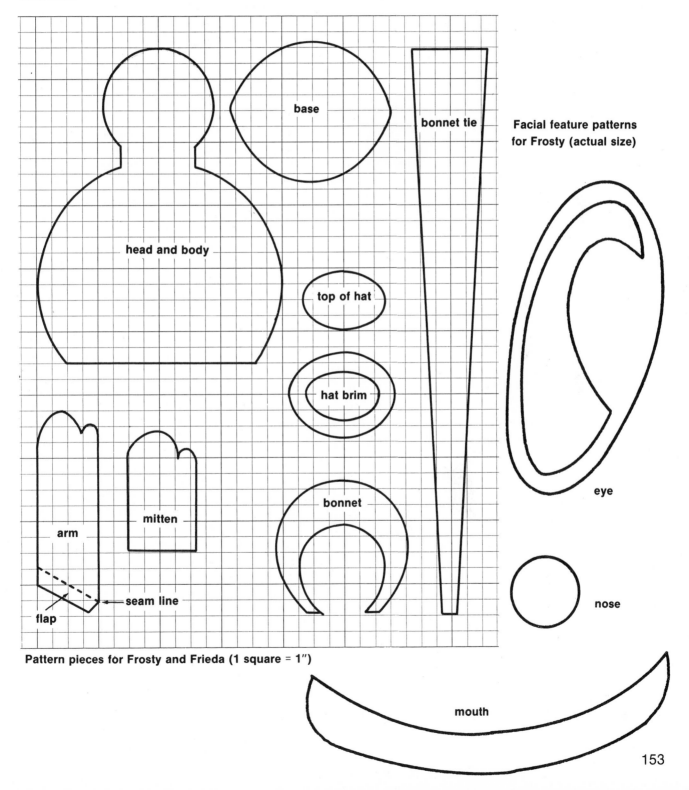

base

bonnet tie

Facial feature patterns for Frosty (actual size)

head and body

top of hat

hat brim

eye

bonnet

mitten

arm

nose

seam line

flap

Pattern pieces for Frosty and Frieda (1 square = 1″)

mouth

Materials for Frieda
- 2/3 yd. 72"-wide white felt
- ¼ yd. 72"-wide red felt
- 10" square of black felt
- ½ oz. silver glitter
- 11" x 22" piece of cardboard
- 1 lb. polyester fiberfill stuffing
- white and red sewing thread
- white glue

To Make Frieda

Enlarge to full size the pattern pieces for Frieda's head and body, arm, and base, and those for her bonnet and bonnet tie (instructions for enlarging are given in Chapter 8). Then trace the pattern pieces for Frieda's facial features. From white felt, cut two head and body pieces, four arms, and one base, following the outlines of the appropriate patterns; from red, four mittens, one mouth, two bonnet pieces, and two bonnet ties, following the outlines of these patterns; and from black, one nose and two eyes, following the patterns, and two circles measuring 1¼ inches in diameter for buttons. Finally, cut one bonnet piece from cardboard, again following the outline of the pattern.

Assemble the body, glue on the facial features, and make the mittens in the same manner as described for Frosty. To make the hat, glue one of the red felt bonnet pieces to each side of the corresponding cardboard piece, sew on the ties, and trim the bonnet with glitter as shown in the photograph. Tack the hat in place on Frieda's head, and form the ties into a big bow. Finally, glue on the buttons, and dress Frieda with her mittens.

Facial feature patterns for Frieda (actual size)

PRETTY GARLAND FOR YOUR TREE

This fringed white garland, trimmed with red and silver, will be something very special on your tree because you've made it yourself. The materials listed here are sufficient for a garland that is 12 yards long. If you wish to make your own garland longer or shorter than this one, simply increase or decrease the amounts used here, remembering that, since the garland will become a little shorter once you've twisted it, you'll need to add 1 or 2 feet to the desired finished length.

Materials
- ¼ yd. 72"-wide white felt
- 24 yds. ¼"-wide bulky red yarn
- 48 yds. ⅛"-wide metallic silver cord
- white sewing thread
- white glue

To Make
Cut the felt into strips 1½ inches wide by a comfortable working length of approximately 1 yard. With pencil, mark off the center ½ inch on one side of each strip. Then cut fine ½-inch-deep fringe along each edge of the strips, cutting up to the pencil marks. Glue the red yarn down the middle of the unclipped center portion of each strip, and glue a length of the silver cord on each side of the yarn. When you've finished one side of the strips, turn them over and trim the other side in the same manner. Finally, sew the strips together end to end, and twist the entire piece as you hang it.

Tree Decorations

While these specially designed tree hangings are traditional in character, they are quite different from any other Christmas creatures you've ever seen—particularly the jaunty Santa Claus mobile and the gleeful Robinson the Reindeer, who looks beside himself with excitement over the holiday. All of these Christmas ornaments are stiffened with cardboard and, except for Santa Claus, are trimmed on one side only and covered with plain white felt on the other. They range in height from approximately 7½ inches to 9 inches.

SANTA CLAUS MOBILE

Materials

- 9" x 12" piece of white felt
- 5" x 12" piece of red felt
- scrap of black felt
- 8" x 10" piece of cardboard
- 2 oz. white medium-weight knitting yarn
- 1 small package of ⅜" red sequins
- small amount of thin gold cord
- white glue

To Make

Trace the Santa Claus pattern and enlarge it to full size (instructions for enlarging are given in Chapter 8). Mark the outline of each of the five separate pieces of the mobile on the cardboard, and then cut out the pieces. Now, using the color key as a guide, mark two of each of the various facial features and portions of the cap on felt scraps of the appropriate color, and cut out all the pieces.

String the cardboard pieces together with gold cord as shown in the photograph, piercing a small hole in each cardboard section and drawing the cord through the hole. To make a hanging loop, pierce a hole near the top of the cap piece, draw an 8-inch length of the gold cord through the hole, and knot the ends together. Glue the felt pieces to each side of the cardboard. Then glue sequins on the nose and the mouth, applying them to both the front and back sides of the pieces.

To make the beard, cut a number of 4-inch lengths of white yarn. Fold them, several layers deep, over the top of the beard piece, and glue them in place. Then cut a number of strands of yarn the length of the moustache, divide the strands into two bundles, tie each bundle together in the middle, and glue one in place on each side of the moustache piece.

Finally, make two 1½-inch white pompons, and glue them to the end of the cap, one on each side of the mobile.

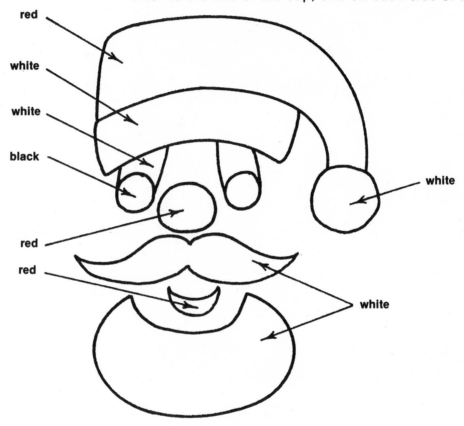

Pattern for Santa Claus mobile (½ actual size)

ROBINSON THE REINDEER

Materials

- 9" x 16" piece of white felt
- scraps of black and red felt
- 8" x 9" piece of cardboard
- several ⅜" red sequins
- small amount of thin gold cord
- white glue

To Make

Trace the pattern for the reindeer and enlarge it to full size (instructions for enlarging are given in Chapter 8). Transfer the outline of the reindeer onto the cardboard and cut the piece out, then cut two pieces of this shape from the white felt. Now, using the color key as a guide, mark two star shapes and one of each of the reindeer's features on felt scraps of the appropriate color, and cut out the pieces.

Glue one of the white felt reindeer shapes in place on each side of the cardboard, then glue all the features in place. Glue the sequins on the nose, and one star at the top of each antler. To hang the reindeer, pierce a small hole near the top of the piece, thread the thin gold cord through the hole, and knot the cord ends together.

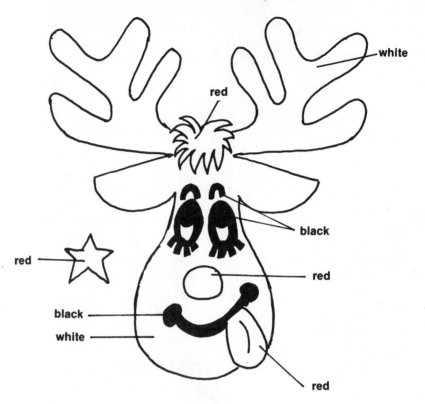

Pattern for Robinson the reindeer (½ actual size)

PRETTY ANGEL

Materials
- 9" x 14" piece of white felt
- 5" x 7" piece of red felt
- scraps of pink and blue felt
- 7" x 9" piece of cardboard
- 10 yds. thin gold cord
- 1 small package of ⅜" red sequins
- 1 small package of ⅜" silver sequins
- 1 yd. narrow metallic silver rickrack
- white glue

To Make

Trace the pattern for the angel and enlarge it to full size (instructions for enlarging are given in Chapter 8). Mark the outline of the angel on the cardboard, and cut out the piece. Then cut two pieces of this shape from the white felt, and using the color key as a guide, mark the outline of the angel's face, features, arms, and the red portions of her gown on felt of the appropriate color, and cut out the pieces.

Glue one of the white felt angel shapes in place on each side of the cardboard. Arrange the other felt pieces on one side of the ornament as shown on the pattern and glue them in place. Glue the rickrack in place on the wings and along each edge of the red panels of the gown as shown in the photograph, then scatter red sequins on the gown and silver sequins on the wings and crown as shown, and glue them in place.

Cut an 8-inch length of gold cord for a hanging cord and set it aside. To make the angel's hair, wind the rest of the gold cord into 4½-inch loops, tie the bundle in the middle, and then shape it to the face and glue it in place. And, to hang the angel, attach the reserved piece of gold cord, piercing a small hole near the top of the piece, drawing the cord through, and knotting the ends together.

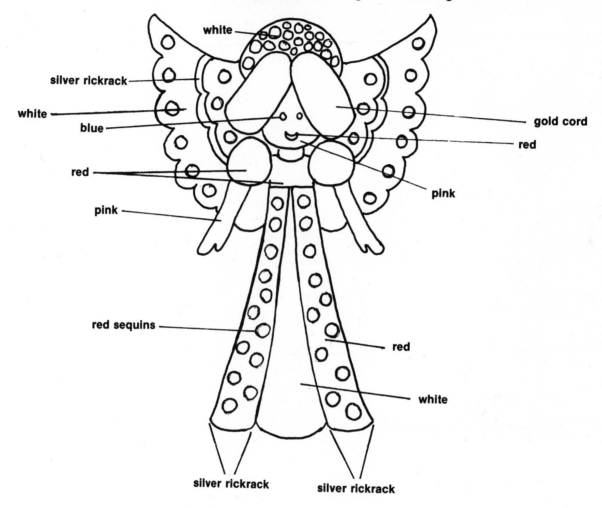

Pattern for angel (½ actual size)

CARROT-NOSED SNOWMAN

Materials

- 9″ x 10″ piece of white felt
- scraps of black and red felt
- 5″ x 9″ piece of cardboard
- 5⅜″ black sequins
- small amount of silver glitter
- small amount of thin gold cord
- white glue

To Make

Trace the pattern for the snowman and enlarge it to full size (instructions for enlarging are given in Chapter 8). Mark the outline of the snowman on the cardboard, and cut out the piece, then cut two pieces of this shape from the white felt; and using the color key as a guide, mark the outline of the snowman's nose, mouth, and scarf on felt scraps of the appropriate color, and cut out the pieces.

Glue one of the white felt snowman shapes in place on each side of the cardboard. Arrange the other felt pieces on one side of the ornament as shown on the pattern, and glue them in place. Using the open tip of the glue bottle, mark the hatband and the wavy lines on the scarf with glue, sprinkling glitter onto the glue as you go. Allow to dry thoroughly, and then gently shake off the excess glitter. Glue the black sequins for the eyes and buttons in place as shown.

To attach a cord to hang the ornament, pierce a small hole near the top of the piece, thread the thin gold cord through the hole, and knot the cord ends together.

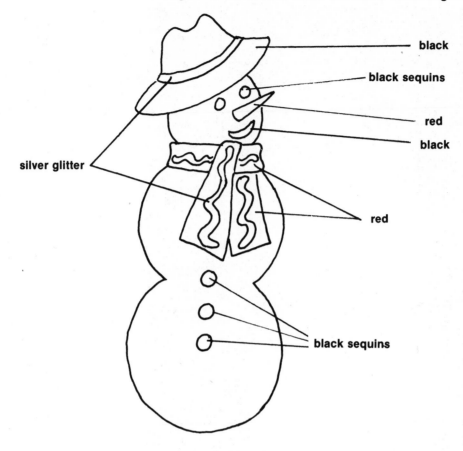

Pattern for snowman (½ actual size)

FANCY GINGERBREAD FOLK

To Make the Gingerbread Lady

Trace the pattern for the gingerbread lady and enlarge it to full size (instructions for enlarging are given in Chapter 8). Mark her outline on the cardboard, and cut out the piece; then from white felt, cut two pieces of the same shape as the cardboard piece, and one 2-inch by 9-inch strip for the skirt; from red, one piece for the mouth and one ¼-inch by 4-inch strip for the bow; and from black, one piece for the nose and two pieces for the eyebrows.

Glue one of the white felt gingerbread lady shapes in place on each side of the cardboard. Arrange the felt pieces for the mouth, nose, and eyebrows, and the two black sequins for the eyes on the face (on one side of the ornament only), and glue them in place. Now, using the pattern as a guide, cut strips of rickrack in appropriate lengths to fit at the wrists, upper arms, neck, and waist, and glue them in place on the ornament as shown.

Materials for the Gingerbread Lady

- 9" x 19" piece of white felt
- scraps of red and black felt
- 8" x 9" piece of cardboard
- 1½ yds. narrow green rickrack
- 1 small package of ⅜" red sequins
- 2 ⅜" black sequins
- small amount of thin gold cord
- white sewing thread
- white glue

To make the skirt, glue a length of rickrack along one long edge of the white felt skirt piece. Run a gathering stitch with sewing thread along the other long edge of the piece, and draw up the thread until the skirt fits the waist. Adjust the gathers evenly and glue the skirt to the figure along the gathered edge only, then glue a strip of rickrack along the waistline to cover the gathering stitches.

To finish, cover the entire bodice with red sequins and glue them in place. Arrange red sequins in polka-dot fashion on the skirt and glue them in place, then shape the narrow red felt strip into a bow, and glue it in place on the bodice as shown on the pattern. Finally, attach a cord to hang the ornament by piercing a hole near the top of the piece, threading the thin gold cord through the hole, and knotting the ends together.

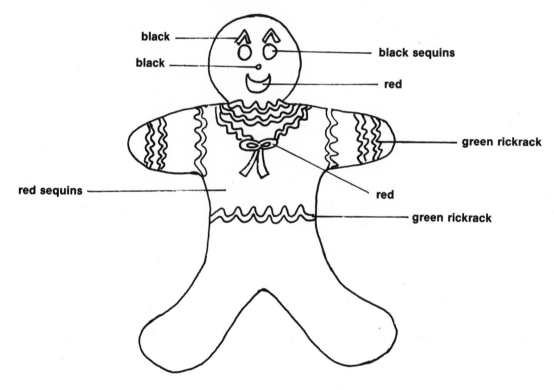

Pattern for gingerbread lady (½ actual size)

To Make the Gingerbread Man

Trace the pattern for the gingerbread man and enlarge it to full size (instructions for enlarging are given in Chapter 8). Then, using the pattern for the gingerbread man, cut and assemble the pieces following the directions for making the gingerbread lady, with these exceptions: eliminate the skirt entirely, outline the vest with gold rickrack as shown on the gingerbread man pattern, cover the vest with green sequins, and use the seven red sequins as buttons.

Materials for the Gingerbread Man
- 9" x 16" piece of white felt
- scraps of red and black felt
- 8" x 9" piece of cardboard
- 1 yd. narrow green rickrack
- ½ yd. narrow metallic gold rickrack
- 1 small package of ⅜" green sequins
- 7 ⅜" red sequins
- 2 ⅜" black sequins
- small amount of thin gold cord
- white glue

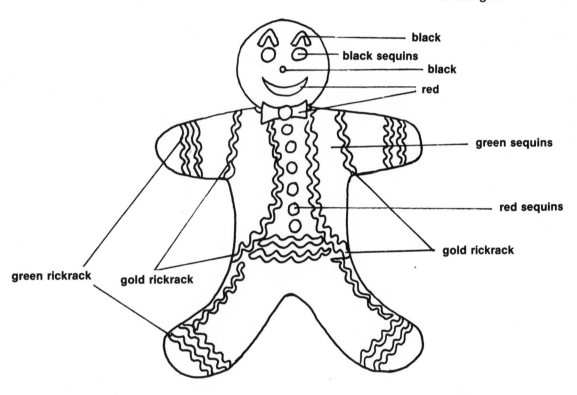

Pattern for gingerbread man (½ actual size)

8.
A GUIDE TO PERFECT WORK

Preparing and Cutting the Material

Enlarging and Reducing a Pattern

Transferring Pattern Markings

Seaming Felt

Appliquéing with Felt

Although working with felt is really so simple that very little special instruction is needed, like all other crafts it does have a few rules that you should be aware of in order to make your experience with it more pleasant and the final results of your work more perfect. The most basic of these rules apply to all crafts: always assemble all the materials, tools, and supplies you will need before you actually begin to make a project, and keep them near at hand as you work; be very careful to measure accurately; and take a little extra time to work neatly.

Beyond these general rules, however, there are some guide lines to follow that apply to any work being done with fabric, and a few that particularly concern the manipulation of felt, which as you know is a material quite different from all others. To help you have the most possible fun with felt, I have included here all the special information you will need to know in order to become adept at this very simple and enjoyable craft.

Preparing and Cutting the Material

Preparing the felt for whatever project you are making is extremely easy. You won't have to straighten the material since it has no grain, although to avoid cutting misshapen or irregular pieces, always press your felt so it is completely smooth and wrinkle-free before you begin to lay out and cut your pattern pieces. To do this work with a steam iron at a wool, or medium, setting and press over a lightly dampened fabric, remembering too to keep the iron in motion to avoid an indentation of it on the material.

When you're ready to lay out your pattern pieces, spread out your felt on a large flat surface—be sure to give yourself enough room to work. Lay out all your pattern pieces before you cut any of them, arranging the largest pieces on the felt first, and fitting the smaller ones into the empty spaces, re-arranging the pieces as often as necessary to be able to get the most out of your yardage, and remembering too that since felt has no grain you can rotate your pattern pieces in any direction necessary.

Having arranged the pattern pieces where you want them on the felt, pin them in place so they won't shift around as you mark or cut them. Now mark the outlines of each pattern piece on the felt by tracing around the edges with a sharp-pointed pencil or a piece of tailor's chalk, then remove the pattern and cut out the piece along the marked outline, or just simply cut out each piece using the edge of the pattern itself as a cutting guide. Whichever method you prefer, it is important to use very sharp scissors and to cut your pieces cleanly and smoothly, since concealed seams and turned-under edges are usually unnecessary with felt, and the way you cut your edges is the way they are likely to be seen when the project is finished.

Enlarging and Reducing a Pattern

Some of the patterns used for projects in this book have been reproduced in the actual size required for the particular project, others will need to be enlarged or, occasionally, reduced in size. To use any of the actual-size patterns, all you have to do is to trace the pattern onto a sheet of tracing paper.

To enlarge or reduce a design to the size you will need for your project, the design must first appear on a graph-paper grid, and many of the patterns in this book are shown this way. However, to prepare a design that isn't shown on a graph, simply trace it onto a sheet of tracing paper, then tape the tracing to a piece of graph paper (four-square-per-inch graph paper is readily available and is a good size to use).

After this has been done, rule a second grid on a large sheet of paper, drawing the squares of this grid in the proportions needed for the size you want the finished pattern to be. If, for example, you've traced a half-size pattern and have taped it to graph paper ruled in ¼-inch squares, to enlarge the pattern to full size you should rule your second grid in ½-inch squares; or if you want to enlarge a pregraphed design that is marked "one square equals 1 inch," rule your new grid in 1-inch squares; and to reduce the size of a design, simply reverse the procedure and draw the squares of your second grid proportionally smaller than the squares of the first grid.

Finally, once you have prepared your enlarged- or reduced-size grid, copy the pattern or design onto it. This may be somewhat time-consuming, especially for a large and detailed design, but it is really quite easy to do if you work square by square. Simply notice where each line of the pattern crosses the lines of a graphed square, mark these points with dots, and then connect the dots. For straight lines, you'll only need to mark a dot where the pattern line enters the square and another dot where it leaves the square; while to shape curved lines more accurately, you may want to mark several intermediate points within the square as well and draw your curved lines between these points.

Transferring Pattern Markings

Several methods may be used to transfer the outlines and internal markings of pattern pieces to the felt. If your full-size design tracing consists of an individual pattern piece for a project—such as the pattern for the quilted mirror frame in Chapter 5 or the pattern for the duck puppet in Chapter 4, the dressmaker's carbon paper and tracing wheel method is an excellent one to use for transferring the outlines and construction details of the pattern to the felt. If, however, the pattern you wish to transfer is a tracing of an entire design and includes several or many pieces that must be cut separately, such as the appliqué trim patterns in Chapter 6, the Christmas tree decorations in Chapter 7, and the wall hangings that appear in several chapters of the book, then you may want to mark your pattern pieces from individual templates rather than working directly from the large tracing.

To transfer pattern markings with a tracing wheel, place a sheet of dressmaker's carbon paper, carbon side down, on the felt, lay the traced pattern on top of it, and go over the lines of the pattern with a tracing wheel. If you don't have a tracing wheel, you can dot your pattern with the point of a very sharp pencil, "stabbing" the markings firmly enough to get a clear carbon imprint on the fabric. Mark your pattern with white dressmaker's carbon paper wherever possible (the white markings usually rub off easily or can be removed with an iron), or use the color closest to that of your felt; and unless you are making lines for topstitching, quilting, embroidery, or other surface detail, it is always advisable to mark on the wrong, rather than the finished, side of the felt.

Making templates takes a little extra time, but there are several advantages to using this method: small and intricate pieces can be marked more easily and accurately, each template can be used over and over again, and instead of chewing up your master design tracing with a tracing wheel you'll be able to preserve it for use as a placement guide for assembling your project. To make templates from your full-size design tracing, retrace each individual part of the larger design onto separate pieces of stiff paper or even lightweight cardboard, and then with a pair of very sharp scissors cut out each piece directly along the outline, or, for a layered look, slightly outside the outline. Thus, for example, if you wanted to make templates for a sunflower design that will have a green stem and leaf, and an orange-petalled flower with a round black center, you would trace the outline of the leaf and stem onto one piece of paper, the petalled part of the flower onto another piece, and the circle for the center of the flower onto a third piece of paper; and then you would cut out each of the individual templates. To use the templates, simply place them on the felt, trace around the edges with a sharp-pointed pencil or a piece of tailor's chalk, remove the templates, and cut out the felt along the marked lines.

Seaming Felt

With most fabrics, seams are usually constructed on the wrong side of the work ½ inch to ⅝ inch in from the edges of the pieces being joined, then they are sewn by machine, or by hand with a backstitch or small running stitch. This method is perfectly appropriate for felt, particularly for making garment seams in areas that will be subject to stress. With our special material, however, other seaming techniques are often preferable because they take advantage of the smooth nonraveling cut edges of the felt and eliminate the bulky seam allowances of ordinary seams. Thus you will find that, for many of the projects in this book, seams are constructed on the right side of the work, and they are made by simply whipstitching the edges together by hand with ⅛-inch-deep stitches, or by topstitching the pieces together ⅛ inch in from the edge. Topstitching can be done by machine or by hand with small, closely spaced running stitches. All hand stitching should be done with slender, sharp-pointed, small-eyed needles; or for machine stitching, use a Size 14 needle. Further, if you wish the seams to be inconspicuous, sew them with self-color thread, or, to create a special design effect, use thread in any contrasting color you wish.

Special design effects can also be created by joining felt pieces with embroidered and crocheted seams. For crochet seams, holes must be punched around the edges of the felt (this is optional for embroidered seams) and, because the holes themselves become a design element, it is important to punch them cleanly and to space them evenly around each edge to be joined—usually ¼ inch apart and ¼ inch in from the edge. And for embroidery work that involves stitching directly into the felt, use a sharp-pointed embroidery or crewel needle in a size just large enough to accommodate your embroidery floss or yarn, or use a blunt-ended tapestry needle for embroidery edging that can be worked through holes punched in the felt.

Appliquéing with Felt

Many of the projects in this book, particularly the patchwork designs and the wall hangings and plaques, are assembled by superimposing one piece of felt on another, and many other projects are trimmed with decorative felt appliqués. Affixing one piece of felt to another can be done by bonding, glueing, or sewing them together, and the instructions for each project specify which of these methods is most appropriate.

Bonding is done by fusing two layers of felt with a piece of fusible bonding material. This weblike material can be purchased in most fabric, department, or chain stores, and comes in sheets and strips of various sizes and lengths, and when using it, it is important to cut the bonding material in the exact same size and shape as the felt appliqué piece you wish to affix (if the bonding material is smaller than the appliqué the edges of the appliqué will remain loose, and if it is larger than the appliqué, the excess may stick to your iron or pressing cloth). Aside from this suggestion, however, there are no special instructions to follow other than those you will find on the package of bonding material.

When project instructions call for glueing felt pieces together, ordinary white household glue is the best type to use. The bottle should be fresh and even-flowing and, when applying the glue, the pointed tip of the container should be held fairly close to the fabric. Apply the glue evenly and use enough to adhere the layers of felt, but not so much that the glue will pucker the material or cake up in spots. Work quickly while you are doing this so you can press the pieces together with the glue still wet, although once you have affixed the appliqué, put the work aside and do not move it for at least fifteen or twenty minutes to allow the glue to set.

Felt appliqué pieces, particularly large ones, can also be applied by the more traditional method of stitching them to the backing fabric. You can sew by hand or by machine, but always work on the right side of the piece and place the stitches ⅛ inch in from the edges of the appliqué. If you prefer to sew by hand, use a slender, sharp-pointed, small-eyed needle; and make small closely spaced running stitches, taking care to leave no gaps and to work evenly and neatly so the stitching will enhance the design.

INDEX